THE
GOLF
SWING
Simplified

JOHN JACOBS

with KEN BOWDEN

Illustrated by
KEN LEWIS

BURFORD BOOKS

Printed in the United States of America
10   9   8   7   6   5
First published in Great Britain by Stanley Paul.

Library of Congress Cataloging-in-Publication Data
Jacobs, John, 1925–
    The golf swing simplified / John Jacobs with Ken Bowden ;
illustrated by Ken Lewis.
        p.   cm.
    ISBN 1-58080-000-9
    1. Swing (Golf).   I. Bowden, Ken.   II. Title.
GV979.S9J33   1994
796.352¢3—dc20   94-17855
                                                        CIP

CONTENTS

PART FOUR: THE SWING

PART FIVE: ANSWERS TO MOST-ASKED QUESTIONS

AUTHORS' NOTE

Even though, to keep the message as simple and clear as the instruction, this book is written from the perspective of the right-handed male golfer, everything in it applies equally to left-handed and women players.

Introduction

They call him the "father of European golf." I call him my friend and mentor. With my ingrained interest and desire to teach, I was fortunate to learn from and partner with one whom many consider to be the best—John Jacobs.

In my formative years, I was an overzealous student of golf's mechanics and swing theory. I sought out all the great teachers of the day, and it seemed the only thing everyone agreed on was that golf was a game of "feel." I became more confused—so much so that I even gave up the game for a while.

Then I found someone who also had studied the game, thoroughly. One who had examined every element of swing mechanics and could translate them into simplified terms—understandable by me and golfers everywhere. As our friendship grew, we formed an alliance that still exists today. John Jacobs' name remains on my worldwide golf schools, nearly 25 years later—born of that early partnership and retained out of respect for sound teaching principles that survive today.

In *The Golf Swing Simplified*, John covers the basics as he has since the early 60s. Ball-striking aspects get the greatest attention, for it is the "cause and effect" that determines the result—the flight of the ball. Excellent illustrations help the student understand the relationship between face, path, and angle of the club at the moment of impact.

Diagnosis, explanation, and correction have been the cornerstone of John's teaching success. He has always been able to know instantly, how the clubhead has met the ball just by watching the ball's flight. It is his basis for a prescription that helps cure faults and teaches the reader how to be his own best teacher.

John's overall ability to be a visionary, in the broader sense, has made him known as "the father of European golf." Through his efforts in teaching, coaching, creating golf practice centers, captaining his Ryder Cup team, and an endless list of other accomplishments, he has driven Britain and Europe into world golf prominence. And continued results, such as John's acknowledged teaching contribution that helped Spaniard Jose Maria Olazabal win the 1994 Masters, support that reputation today.

Since 1971, Jacobs' *Practical Golf* has been the hallmark of golf instruction books. Today, *The Golf Swing Simplified* makes his philosophies even more understandable, a must for every student of the game.

—Shelby Futch
   Founder, President, CEO
   John Jacobs' Golf Schools

PART ONE

Golf's True Fundamentals

CHAPTER 1

The golf swing's only purpose

The majority of the world's 35 million golfers never play the game as well as they could because they have no idea, an incorrect idea, or an incomplete idea of what they are trying to do when they swing a golf club.

The golf swing has only one purpose: **to deliver the head of the club to the ball correctly**.

BEN HOGAN

JACK NICKLAUS

SEVE BALLESTEROS

How that is done is immaterial, so long as the method used permits correct impact to be achieved over and over and over again.

BEN HOGAN

JACK NICKLAUS

SEVE BALLESTEROS

CHAPTER 2

Golf's only 'secret'

The behaviour of the golf ball is determined solely by four impact factors interacting with each other. They are:

1. The direction in which the face of the club looks, or the **clubface alignment**.

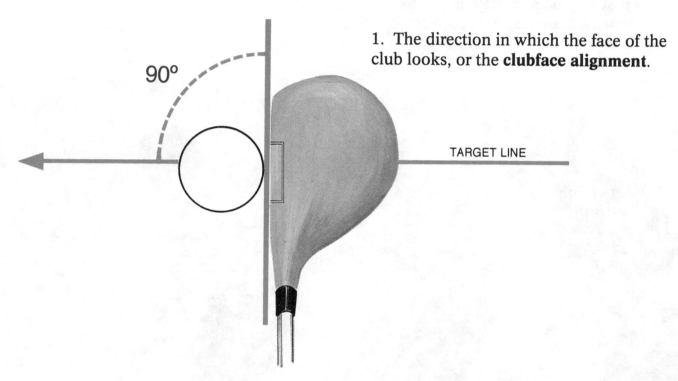

TARGET LINE

90°

2. The direction in which the clubhead travels, or the **path of the swing**.

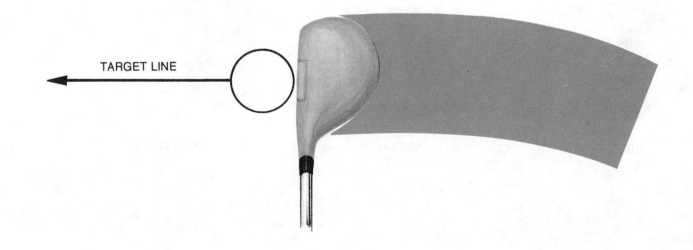

TARGET LINE

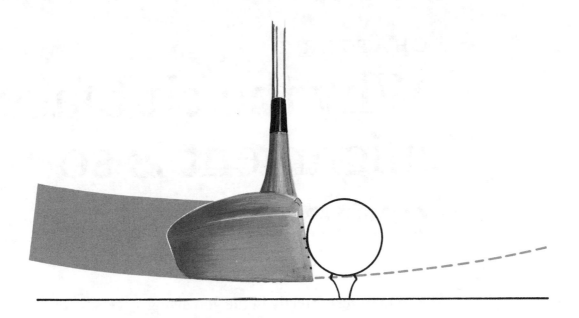

3. The angle of inclination at which the clubhead arrives at the ball, or the **angle of attack**.

4. The **speed** of the clubhead.

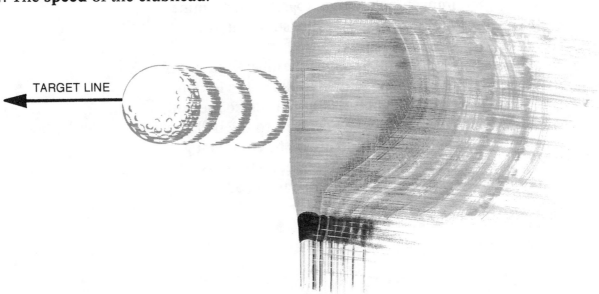

TARGET LINE

Everything you do in swinging a golf club should be related to these all-important impact factors.

Getting them right is golf's only 'secret'.

CHAPTER 3

Why the clubface alignment is so critical

Do one thing correctly in the golf swing and it produces correctness in other areas. Do something incorrectly and the error creates incorrectness elsewhere. In that sense, golf is a **reaction** game. Keep that uppermost in your mind in all your practice and play.

In this regard, **the alignment of the clubface** is the most important of the four impact factors that, together, determine the behaviour of every shot you hit.

Clubface alignment is critical because, if the face of the club looks to the left or right of your target as you strike the ball, your instinctive reactions to the ball's flight **will create errors in your swing path and angle of attack, while also impairing your clubhead speed**.

BALL FLIGHT

CLUBFACE OPEN

TARGET LINE

CHAPTER 4

When the clubface looks right of target

Delivering the clubface looking to the right of the target at impact – or 'open' in golfing terminology – promotes swinging the clubhead from **outside to inside** across the target line in an instinctive attempt to prevent shots from finishing to the right.

Swinging across the target line from out to in can create either a too **steep** (downward) or too **shallow** (upward) hit. This incorrect angle of attack results in both 'fat' or 'thin' contact.

Thirdly, the awkwardness resulting from a sense of incorrect angles inhibits free and forceful swinging, which reduces clubhead speed.

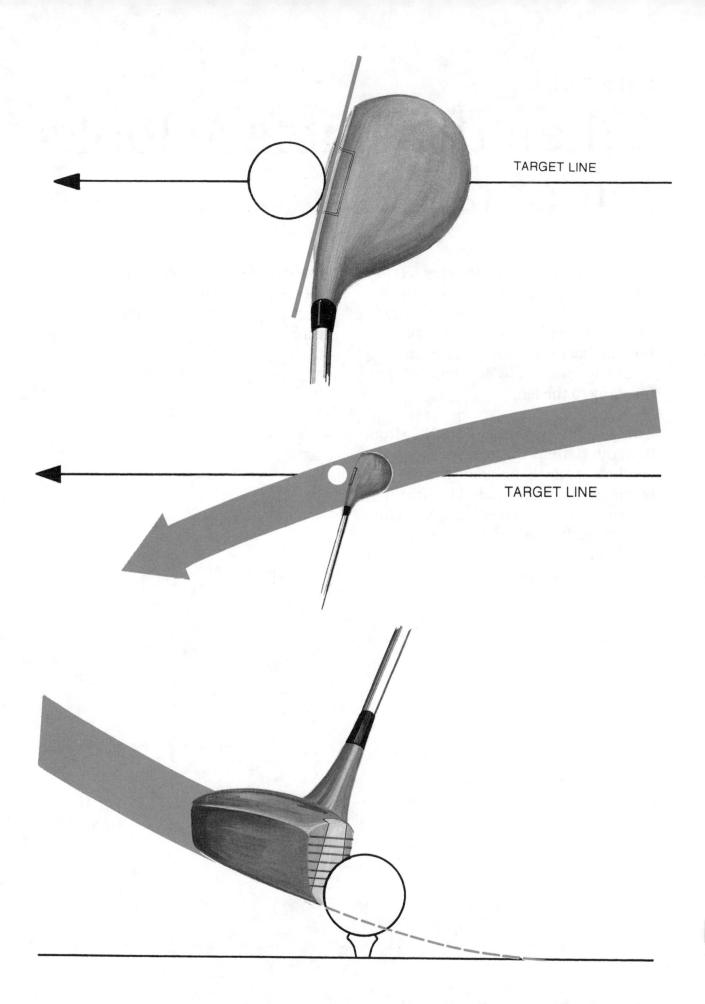

TARGET LINE

TARGET LINE

CHAPTER 5

When the clubface looks left of target

Delivering the clubface **looking left** of the target at impact – or 'closed' in golfing terminology – promotes swinging the clubhead across from the **inside to the outside** of the target line in an instinctive attempt to prevent shots from finishing to the left.

Swinging the clubhead excessively from in to out **flattens** the angle of the clubhead's attack, frequently to the point where it strikes the ground before the ball or has begun travelling upward at impact, again producing either 'fat' or 'thin' contact.

As with the open clubface at impact, awkwardness resulting from a sense of incorrect angles reduces clubhead speed by inhibiting free and forceful swinging.

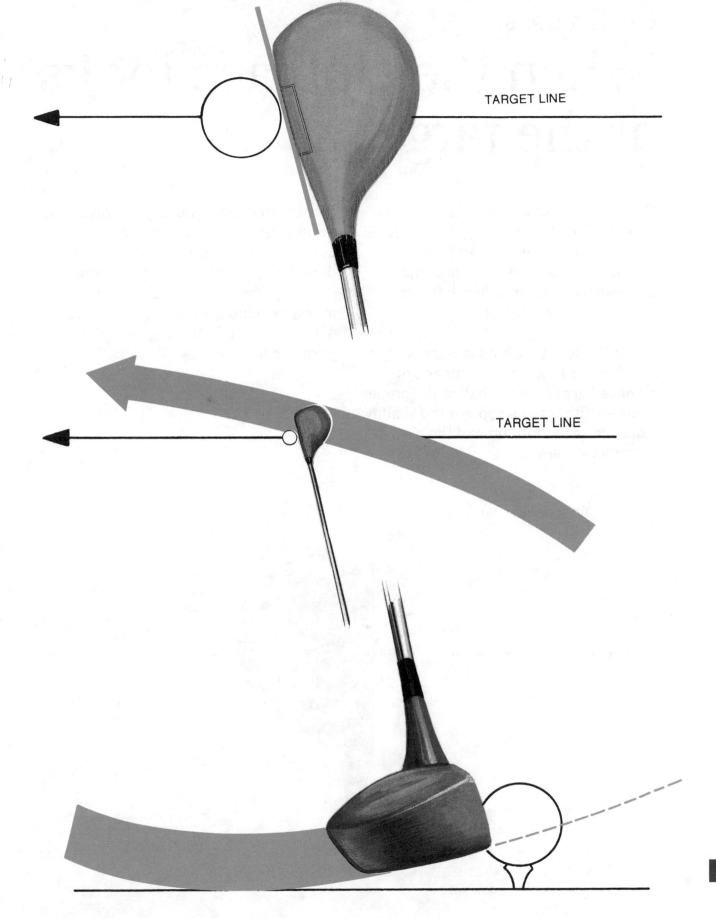

TARGET LINE

TARGET LINE

CHAPTER 6

When the clubface looks at the target

Delivering the clubface to the ball looking directly at the target – or 'square' in golfing terminology – promotes instinctively swinging the clubhead **momentarily along** rather than across the target line at impact.

When the swing path momentarily matches the target line at impact, the clubhead arrives at the ball at the proper angle – neither too steep nor too shallow – delivering the full force of the blow **directly forward**.

Sensing that the 'geometry' is correct in every dimension, and that the ball in consequence will go in the desired direction, promotes free and forceful swinging, thereby producing both maximum clubhead speed and distance with every club in the bag, as well as great accuracy.

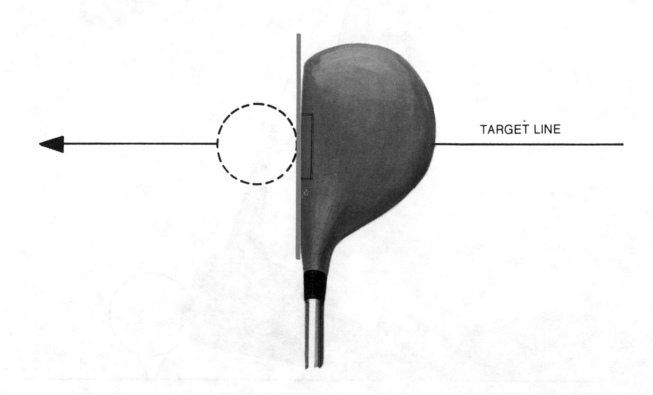

TARGET LINE

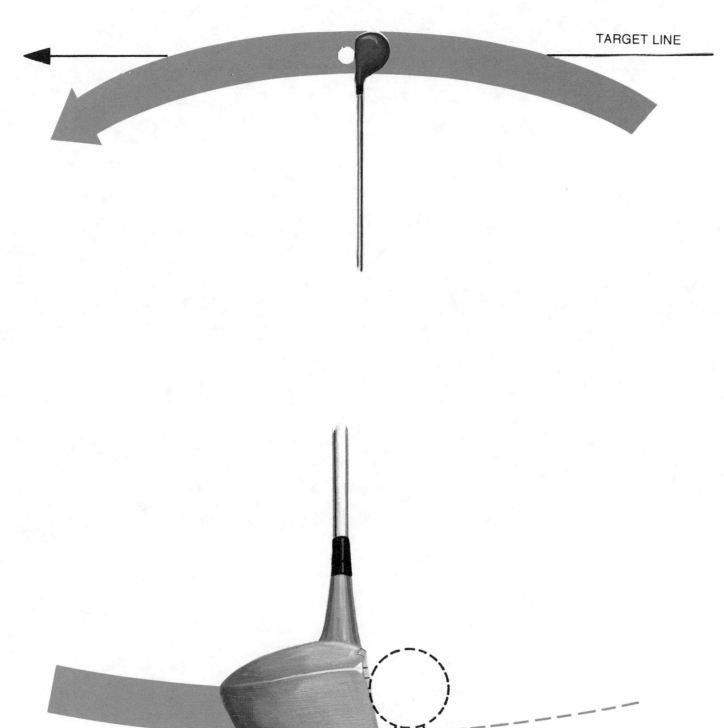

WHEN THE CLUBFACE LOOKS AT THE TARGET

PART TWO

The 'Geometry' of Golf

STRAIGHT
- CLUBFACE SQUARE
- CLUBHEAD SWING PATH IN-TO-SQUARE-TO-
- CORRECT ANGLE OF ATTACK
- BALL FLIES STRAIGHT

HOOK
- CLUBFACE CLOSED
- CLUBHEAD SWING PATH IN-TO-OUT
- SHALLOW ANGLE OF ATTACK
- BALL STARTS RIGHT, THEN CURVES LEFT

PULL
- CLUBHEAD SQUARE TO SWING PATH
- CLUBHEAD SWING PATH OUT-TO-IN
- STEEP ANGLE OF ATTACK
- BALL FLIES STRAIGHT LEFT

PULLED HOOK
- CLUBHEAD CLOSED TO THE SWING PATH
- CLUBHEAD SWING PATH OUT-TO-IN
- STEEP ANGLE OF ATTACK
- BALL STARTS LEFT, THEN CURVES FURTHER LEFT

THE FLIGHT OF THE BALL TELLS ALL

22

SLICE
- CLUBFACE OPEN
- CLUBHEAD SWING PATH OUT-TO-IN
- STEEP ANGLE OF ATTACK
- BALL STARTS LEFT, THEN CURVES RIGHT

PUSH
- CLUBHEAD SQUARE TO SWING PATH
- CLUBHEAD SWING PATH IN-TO OUT
- SHALLOW ANGLE OF ATTACK
- BALL FLIES STRAIGHT RIGHT

PUSHED SLICE
- CLUBFACE OPEN TO THE SWING PATH
- CLUBHEAD SWING PATH IN-TO-OUT
- SHALLOW ANGLE OF ATTACK
- BALL STARTS RIGHT, THEN CURVES FURTHER RIGHT

CHAPTER 7

The flight of the ball tells all

We have seen that the behaviour of every golf shot is determined not by how the club is swung – by the form of bodily motions employed – but by how each swing **delivers the clubface to the ball**.

However, everything is moving much too fast for the golfer to see what is happening on impact. How, then, can he discover the alignment of the clubface, the path of the swing, the angle of attack, and the speed of the clubhead?

The answer is: **the flight of the ball**.

The single most important step in becoming a good golfer is the first one we dealt with: knowing what you should be trying to do with the club by learning and accepting the game's true fundamentals – the correct 'geometry' of impact.

The next most important step is acquiring the knowledge that enables you to identify what's happening at impact from the flight of your shots.

Master those two mental disciplines and your eventual playing ability becomes solely a matter of how hard you are willing and able to work at golf. Ignore or short-change them in your urge to get on with swinging the club and hitting the ball, and you will forever play below your innate potential.

The 'geometry' of golf is set out in the following pages as clearly and graphically as I know how. If you gain nothing else from this book, learn it well and use it wisely.

CHAPTER 8

When the clubhead swings from out to in

THE SLICE: ball starts left of target line then curves right

The swing path is from *out to in* across the target line.

The clubface looks to the right of or is open to the swing path, resulting in an oblique or 'cutting' impact with the ball that creates clockwise sidespin.

As the ball's forward momentum decreases, the clockwise sidespin curves the ball more and more to the right.

The more open the clubface and/or the more out to in the swing path, the stronger the sidespin and the more pronounced the slice.

Also, the more out to in the clubhead path, the steeper the angle of attack, thus the more oblique the impact in a perpendicular as well as a horizontal plane.

The combination of clockwise sidespin and additional backspin produced by the open clubface and/or the steep angle of attack make this the weakest shot in golf, flying excessively high if the ball is contacted at the bottom of the arc, or excessively low if the bottom of the arc is sufficiently forward for the ball to be 'thinned' or 'topped'.

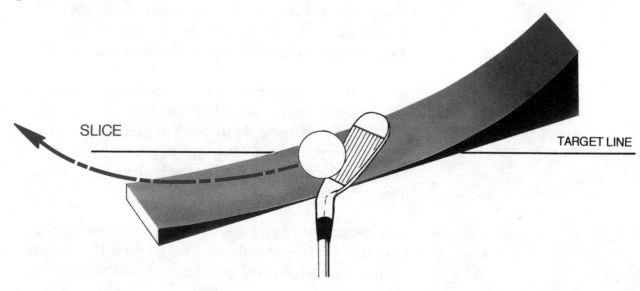

SLICE

TARGET LINE

THE PULL: ball flies straight but left of target

The swing path is from *out to in* across the target line.

The clubface is square to the swing path, but closed to the target line.

Because the clubhead path and clubface alignment 'match', the impact is flush rather than oblique. Thus good distance is obtained.

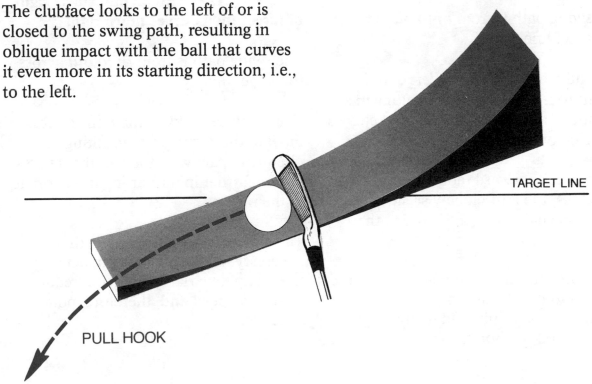

TARGET LINE

PULL

THE PULLED HOOK: ball starts left of target line then curves more left

The swing path is from *out to in* across the target line.

The clubface looks to the left of or is closed to the swing path, resulting in oblique impact with the ball that curves it even more in its starting direction, i.e., to the left.

At its worst, this shot is literally 'smothered', to the extent that the ball fails to rise sufficiently off the ground to go any appreciable distance.

TARGET LINE

PULL HOOK

CHAPTER 9

When the clubhead swings from in to out

THE PUSH: ball flies straight but right of target

The swing path is from *in to out* across the target line.

The clubface is square to the swing path, but *open* to the *target line*.

Because the clubhead path and clubface alignment 'match,' the impact is flush rather than oblique and good distance is obtained.

THE HOOK: ball starts right of target then curves left

The swing path is from *in to out* across the target line.

The clubface looks to the *left* of or is *closed* to the swing path, resulting in an oblique contact with the ball that creates anti-clockwise sidespin.

As the ball's forward momentum decreases, the anti-clockwise sidespin curves the ball more and more to the left.

The more closed the clubface and/or the more in to out the swing path, the stronger the sidespin and the more pronounced the hook.

Also, the more in to out the clubhead path, the shallower the angle of attack, thus the greater the risk of the clubhead catching the ground before the ball, resulting in either 'fat' or 'thin' contact.

Assuming clean back-of-the-ball impact, the combination of lower flight and additional roll resulting from a *slightly* closed clubface and a *slightly* in to out clubhead path – ie a draw as opposed to a full-blooded hook (see next chapter) – produces more distance for a given amount of clubhead speed than any other impact configuration.

THE PUSHED SLICE: ball starts right of target then curves more right

The swing path is from *in to out* across the target line.

The clubface looks to the *right* of or is *open* to the swing path, resulting in oblique impact with the ball that curves it even farther in its starting direction, ie, to the right.

The type of in-to-out swing path necessary to produce this impact 'geometry' invariably results in reduced clubhead speed and, therefore, poor distance.

It should be noted, as an aside, that today's excessive fear of swinging 'over the top' – a fault to be discussed later – makes this type of shot very common at most levels of the game. The cure lies in allowing the clubface to square automatically at impact by swinging the clubhead through the ball from 'in to in' relative to the target line (see next chapter).

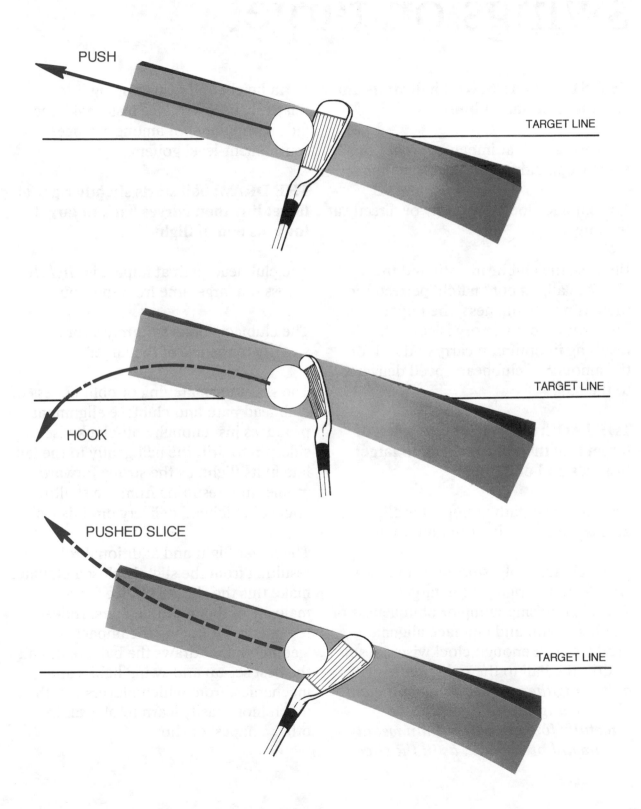

CHAPTER 10

When the clubhead swings on target

THE STRAIGHT SHOT: ball starts and continues on target line

The swing path at impact *matches* or exactly coincides with the target line.

The clubface looks *squarely* or directly at the target.

Because the clubhead path and the clubface alignment 'match' perfectly, ie, there is no obliqueness, the impact is flush, and the trajectory is correct, resulting in optimum carry and roll for the amount of clubhead speed delivered to the ball.

THE FADE: ball starts slightly left of target line then curves back to target towards end of flight

The clubhead path at impact is *slightly* across the target line from out to in.

The clubface looks *squarely* at or *very slightly* to the right of the target.
The slight mismatching or obliqueness of clubhead path and clubface alignment produces just enough clockwise sidespin to drift the ball to the right, *while delivering the clubhead at a sufficiently shallow angle for the blow to be forcefully forward rather than weakly downward or upward, as in the slice.*

Extra height and fast stopping, for relatively little distance loss, make the fade a popular shot among stronger tournament-level golfers.

THE DRAW: ball starts slightly right of target line then curves back to target towards end of flight

The clubhead path at impact is *slightly* across the target line from in to out.

The clubface looks *squarely* at or *very slightly* to the left of the target.

The slight mismatching or obliqueness of clubhead path and clubface alignment produces just enough anti-clockwise sidespin to drift the ball gently to the left late in its flight, as the strong forward momentum resulting from the shallow angle of clubhead delivery diminishes.

The lower flight and additional roll resulting from the slightly closed clubface make this the shot of choice for the majority of the world's golfers. Indeed, repeatedly producing the impact 'geometry' that draws the ball creates all the best set-up and swing habits and mechanics, from which players can then much more easily learn to play all the other 'shapes' of shot.

STRAIGHT

TARGET LINE

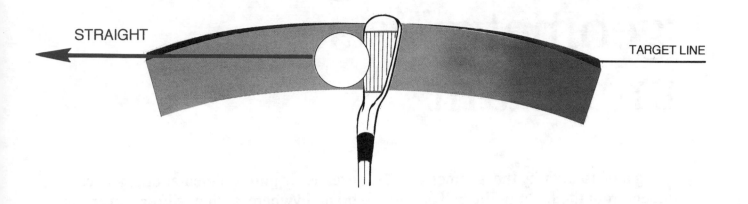

FADE

TARGET LINE

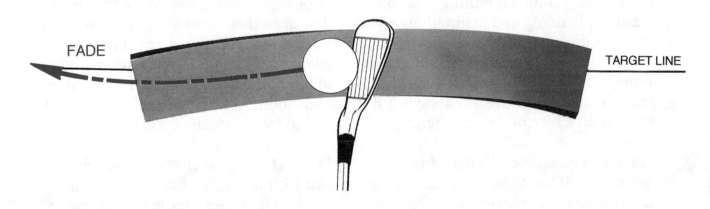

TARGET LINE

DRAW

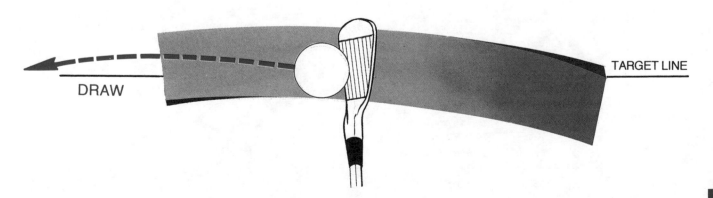

CHAPTER 11

Why knowing golf's 'geometry' is so important

Being able to identify the 'geometry' of impact from the flight of the ball is fundamental to playing golf up to your maximum potential.

Given that ability, everything you do in learning, building and maintaining a golf swing is directed towards achieving the game's number one fundamental: **correct impact**. Without that ability, each swing lacks focus; occurs in a vacuum; is little more than a hit-and-hope experiment.

Once you completely understand the 'geometry' of the game, all you have to do to analyse your swing – to decide how to correct it or improve it – is **to think about the way the golf ball reacts when you hit it**. And, because that

exercise is purely a mental one, you can do it anywhere: sitting at home, even, as well as on the golf course or driving range.

Pupils are amazed that, once they have described their basic shot patterns to me, I can give them a lesson over the telephone. The reason is that the **flight of the ball** tells mc everything I need to know both to diagnose their swing faults and to formulate the cure.

The flight of your shots will provide you with that information also, if only you will let it. And letting it will make golf a much easier game than you ever believed possible.

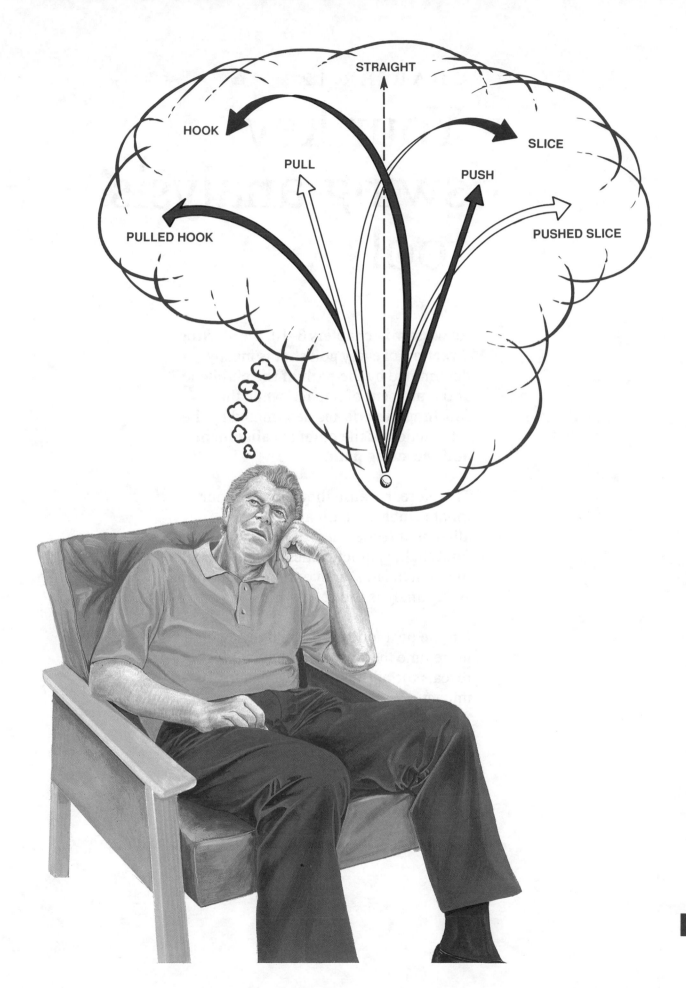

CHAPTER 12

Your key swing-analysis tools

As we saw in chapters 8–10, the **starting direction** of every golf shot is mostly determined by the **path of the clubhead** at the moment of impact; while the **finishing direction** is determined by the inter-action of the **clubface alignment and the swing path**.

Therefore, because they indicate your innate clubhead path and clubface alignment tendencies, the **initial** and the **final** flight characteristics of your most frequent 'misses' are your most important swing analysis tools.

On the next four pages we'll review one more time the ways in which ball flight reveals the all-important 'geometry' of impact.

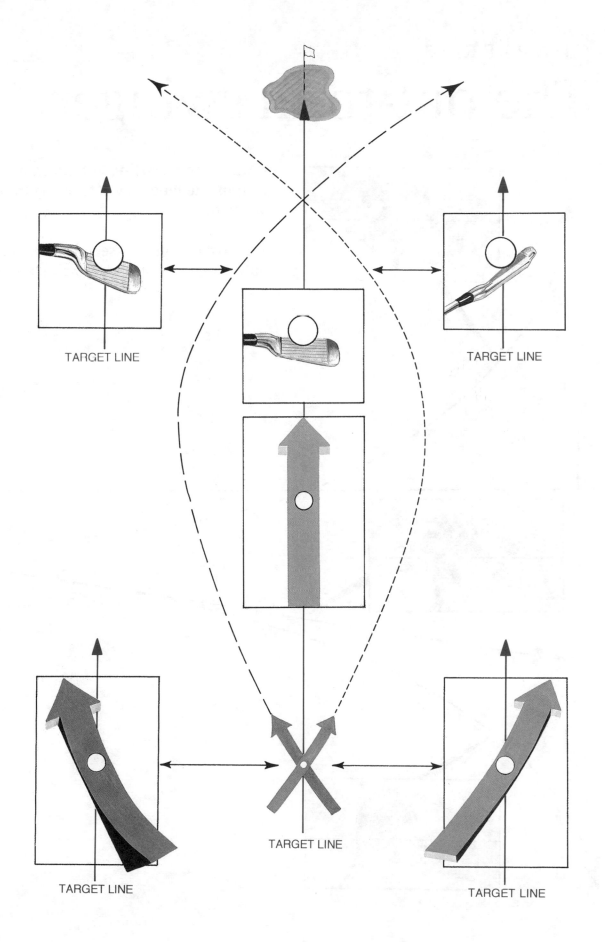

TARGET LINE

TARGET LINE

TARGET LINE

TARGET LINE

TARGET LINE

CHAPTER 13

The out-to-in swinger

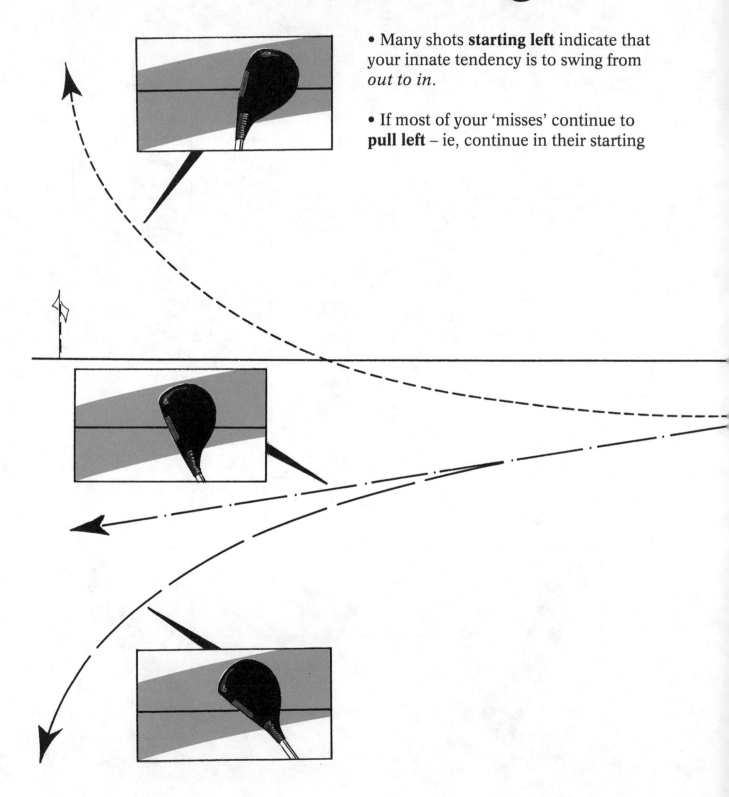

• Many shots **starting left** indicate that your innate tendency is to swing from *out to in*.

• If most of your 'misses' continue to **pull left** – ie, continue in their starting direction – your clubface is *closed* to your target line, even though it is square to your swing path.

• If many of your shots **slice far to the right**, your *out-to-in* swing path is accompanied by a *wide-open* clubface at impact.

• If the majority of your shots **fade** only a little to the right, you are delivering the clubface to the ball *slightly open*.

• If some shots **start left** of your target line, then **hook even more left**, you are delivering the clubface *closed* to your swing path and even *more closed* to your target line.

• Because heavily-lofted irons impart little if any sidespin (see chapter 15), the direction of shots hit with them will confirm your out-to-in swing-path tendencies, ie, the ball will mostly be pulled straight left.

CHAPTER 14
The in-to-out swinger

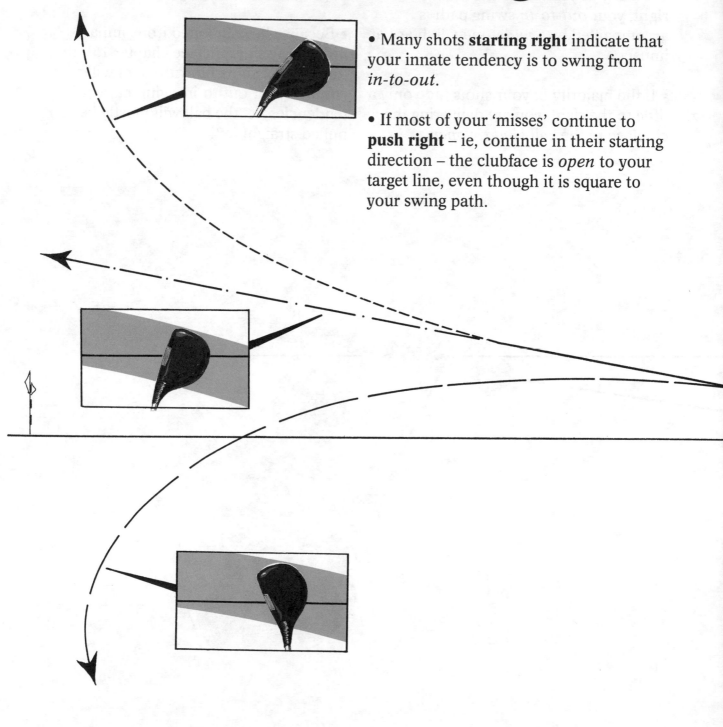

• Many shots **starting right** indicate that your innate tendency is to swing from *in-to-out*.

• If most of your 'misses' continue to **push right** – ie, continue in their starting direction – the clubface is *open* to your target line, even though it is square to your swing path.

• If many of your shots **hook far to the left**, your *in-to-out* swing path is accompanied by a *very closed* clubface at impact.

• If the majority of your shots **draw** only a little to the left, you are delivering the clubface to the ball in a *slightly closed* alignment.

• If some shots **start right** of your target line, then **slice even more right**, you are delivering the clubface *open* to your swing path and *even more open* to your target line.

• Because heavily-lofted irons impart little if any sidespin (see next chapter), the direction of shots hit with them will confirm your in-to-out swing-path tendencies, ie, you will mostly push the ball straight right. However, because closing the clubface reduces its effective loft, you may also sometimes hook the ball with the short-irons.

CHAPTER 15

Confirming your tendencies

Still not entirely sure of your innate swing tendencies? Here's how to find out.

The less lofted the face of a golf club, the less backspin it imparts to the ball (which, of course, is why a long-iron flies so much lower than a pitching-wedge).

The less backspin the ball carries, the more sidespin imparted to it by obliqueness or mismatching of clubhead path and clubface alignment causes it to curve in flight.

For a true reading of your **clubface alignment** at impact, therefore, hit some shots with your *driver*. Any curvature indicates how you tend to deliver the clubface at impact: looking right of target (open) if the shots mostly curve to the right; looking left of target (closed) if the shots mostly curve to the left.

To assess your **clubhead path**, hit some shots with your *9-iron*. Because the strong backspin created by its steeply-pitched face negates most of any sidespin imparted to the ball, the shots will continue to fly in their starting direction with little or no curvature. If they mostly start to the left, your clubhead path obviously is from out to in. If they mostly

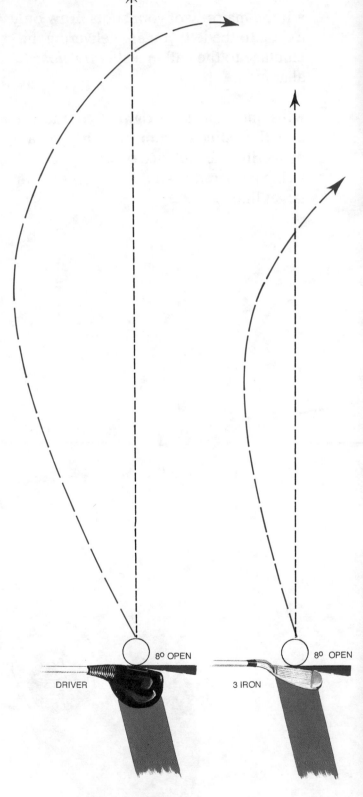

start to the right, you are equally obviously swinging from in to out.

The inter-action of backspin and sidespin is the answer, of course, to one of golf's great mysteries for many golfers: 'Why do my driver shots finish to the right and my short-irons to the left of my target?'

The truth is that the attack on the ball – *out to in and open-faced* – remains constant, while the countering of sidespin by increasing backspin as the clubs become more lofted simply disguises the clubface error.

In short, just another example of golf's single most important fundamental:

The flight of the ball ALWAYS tells you EVERYTHING you need to know to become a better player.

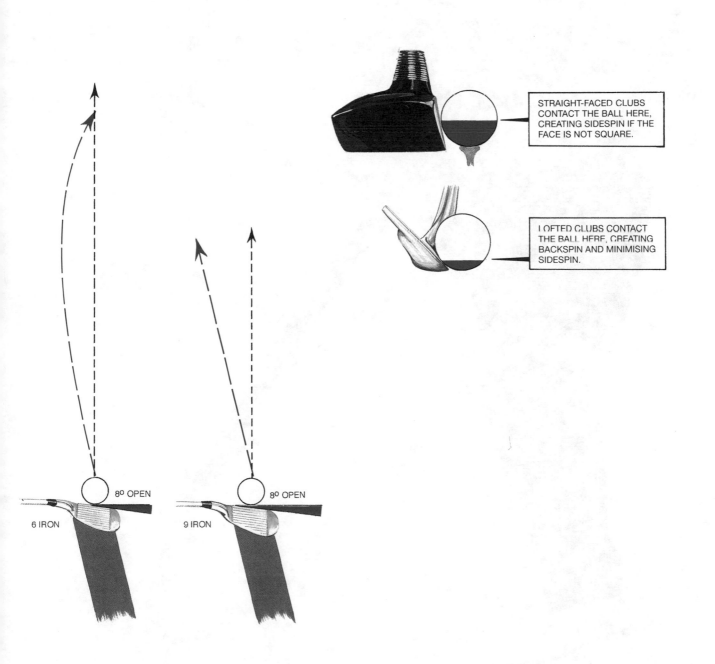

STRAIGHT-FACED CLUBS CONTACT THE BALL HERE, CREATING SIDESPIN IF THE FACE IS NOT SQUARE.

LOFTED CLUBS CONTACT THE BALL HERE, CREATING BACKSPIN AND MINIMISING SIDESPIN.

8º OPEN

8º OPEN

6 IRON

9 IRON

CHAPTER 16
Achieving correct impact – I

ACHIEVING CORRECT IMPACT – I

40

The last element of 'geometry' to burn deep into your golfing consciousness concerns the **clubhead path** necessitated by the fact that, in order to swing a golf club freely and forcefully, you have no alternative but to stand *to one side of the ball*.

Another way to put this is that the golfer is always located **inside the arc** he causes the clubhead to describe during the swing.

That being the case, for the head of the club to be swung momentarily directly along the target line at impact, it *must* travel from the golfer's side of that line – ie, from **inside** the target line – right up to the instant it strikes the ball. Should the clubhead pass beyond or to the

outside of the target line before that instant, there is no way it can be swung along the target line at impact, but only back across it from **out to in**.

For the same reason – ie, you are standing within the swing arc – the clubhead, unless misdirected by some kind of manipulation, will begin to swing to the **inside** of the target line again **as soon as the ball has been struck**.

Thus the clubhead path of a golf swing that hits the ball straight is not, as so many weaker players seem to believe, from in to out, but:

From inside, to momentarily straight through, to inside again.

CHAPTER 17

Achieving correct impact – II

One of the most common faults I see as a teacher is of players swinging the club-head on **too straight a path**, relative to the target line, both back from and down to and through the ball, in the mistaken belief that this will promote straighter-flying shots. What it actually does is severely inhibit square and speedy application of the clubface to the ball.

So let me reinforce what we have just learned about achieving the correct swing path, and at the same time prepare us to move on to swing technique, by looking at its 'geometry' from a slightly different perspective.

The most anatomically effective way – in terms of both force and accuracy – to

strike an object lying on the ground to one side of us is by swinging our arms **back and up** as our body **rotates** away from the target, then **down and through** as our body **rotates** back towards the target.

When allowed to respond naturally to those relatively simple motions, the head of a golf club swings progressively **to** the inside of the target line during the backswing; then progressively **from** the inside of the target line on its way back to the ball; then at impact **momentarily directly along the target line**; then progressively **back again to the inside** of the target line.

Assuming we don't artificially manipulate the face of the club during that process, it begins progressively to **open** relative to the target line, and continues to do so to the completion of the backswing; then, on its way back to the ball, reverses that process, gradually **closing** until it arrives at impact perfectly **square**; then begins to **close** again and goes on doing so to the completion of the follow-through.

How do we assure correctness in all of those areas?

The answers to that question will comprise most of the rest of this book.

PART THREE

Preparing to swing

CHAPTER 18

Your grip controls your clubface alignment

Grip your clubs correctly and you are *50 per cent of the way to playing golf up to your maximum potential*. Grip them incorrectly and, irrespective of how much time and effort you devote to the game, you will *always* play less well than you are capable of doing.

Why is your grip so important? The answer is:

On every shot you hit, from a drive to a chip, **the positioning and pressure of your hands on the club control where its face looks when it meets the ball.***

What is a 'correct' grip? The answer is:

The grip that enables *you* – not, note, Nick Faldo or Seve Ballesteros, or anyone else whose game you admire, but *you* – **to face the club in the direction you are swinging it, at impact, at speed, repetitively.**

How do you find and make a habit of such a grip? The answer is:

By intelligent trial and error within certain well-proven principles, applying whatever amounts of patience and perseverance are necessary to overcome any frustrations or discomforts involved. *In the latter regard, you should know that, in over 40 years of teaching golf, I have yet to encounter a good golfer with a bad grip or a bad golfer with a good grip.*

Over centuries of golf, a particular pattern of positioning the hands on the club has been found to make swinging its face squarely through the ball, at speed, repetitively, easiest for the majority of players. We'll look at that basic starting pattern first, then at the variations you may need to make to find your own correct grip.

* If you need a refresher on the importance of clubface alignment, re-read chapters 3–6.

47

CHAPTER 19

Gripping with your left hand

Lay the club diagonally across your open left hand, so that it lies in the crook of the first finger and across the base of the palm under the thumb pad.

Close the hand so that the thumb rides just to the right side of the shaft and the last three fingers hold the shaft snugly against your palm.

When you now ground the club with its face looking squarely at your target, the 'V' formed by the thumb and forefinger of the left hand should point midway between your nose and your right shoulder extremity. Looking straight down at this hand, you should be able to see at least one but no more than three of its knuckles.

The size and flexibility of your hands will determine precisely how the club nestles into the palm and fingers of your left hand. Seek a sensation of the last three fingers pressing the shaft securely but not tightly against the fleshy underside of the thumb pad.

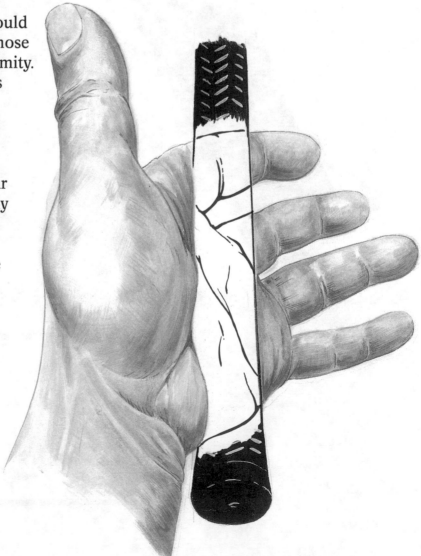

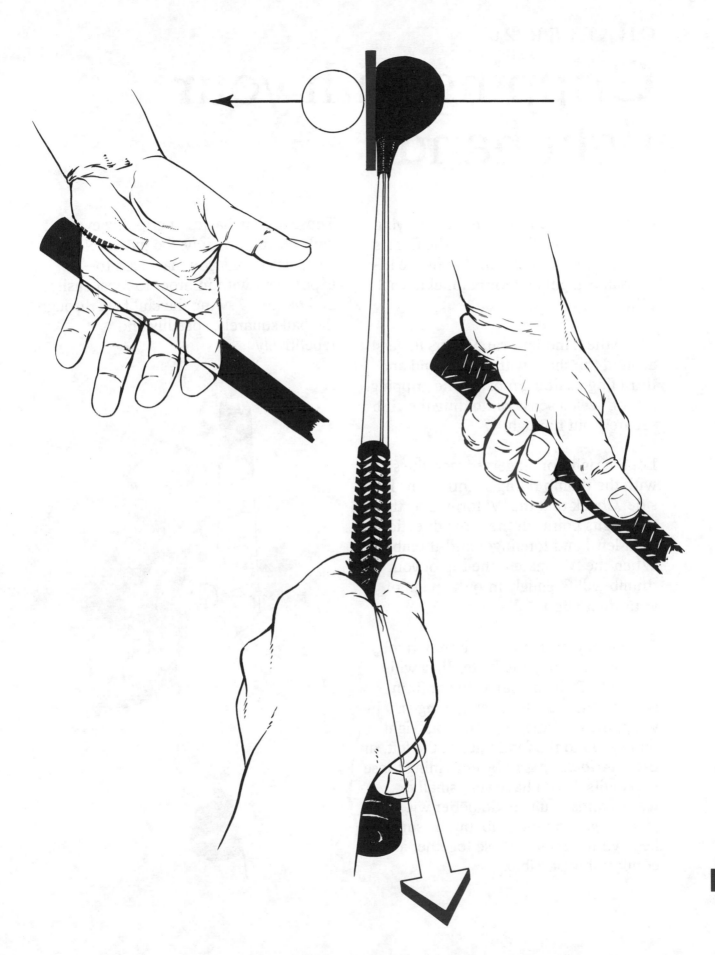

CHAPTER 20

Gripping with your right hand

Begin to add your right hand by laying the shaft across the roots of the fingers so that the backs of both hands are in the same alignment, or parallel to each other.

Close the hand by wrapping its fingers around the shaft, with the second and third fingers doing most of the gripping. Again, seek a sense of holding the club securely but not tightly.

Let the right forefinger 'trigger' the shaft, with the thumb riding slightly to its left side. Check that the 'V' formed by these two digits points in the same direction as your left-hand forefinger-and-thumb 'V.' When the 'Vs' match, the top of your left thumb will fit snugly into the palm of your right hand.

The more your hands work in harmony during the swing, the better they will function. To help 'marry' them, form what is know as the *overlapping grip* by wrapping the little finger of your right hand around the forefinger of the left, or the *interlocking grip* by entwining those two digits. If you have very small or weak hands you may do better with all eight fingers on the club, but be sure to keep your hands as close together as is comfortably possible.

Those are the basics of gripping every club except, possibly, the putter. Next, some variations you may need to experiment with in order to most easily and naturally swing the clubface through the ball squarely, speedily and repetitively.

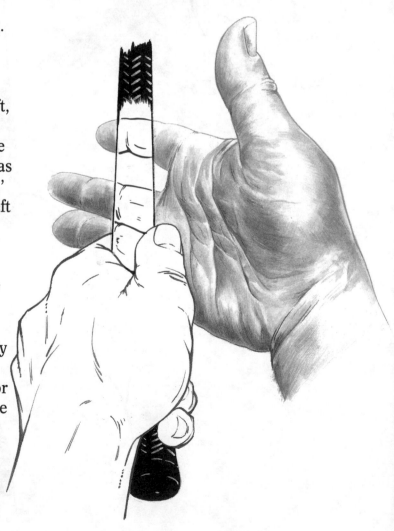

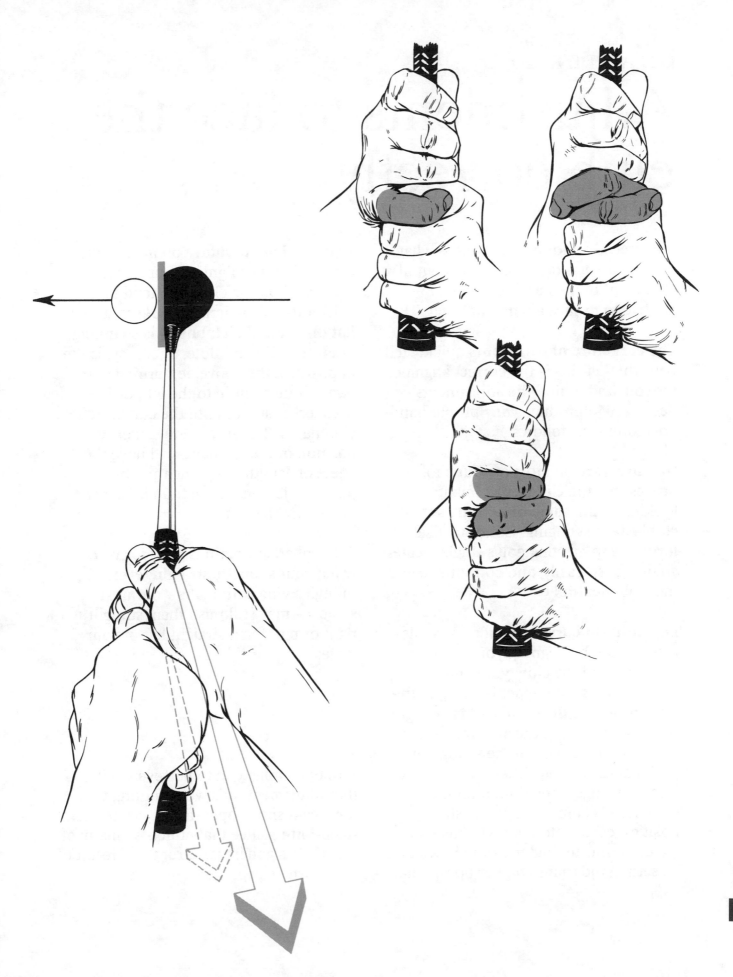

CHAPTER 21

Adjustments to face the club correctly

The preceding formula produces what in golfing terms is described as a 'neutral' alignment of the hands on the club relative to its face alignment.

The **curvature of your shots** quickly tells you whether this is the correct alignment for you, and, if not, the adjustments necessary to produce *your* proper hand positioning, as follows:

No curvature on most of your shots proves that the clubface at impact is looking in **the same direction** as the clubhead is swinging. Count yourself fortunate in meeting golf's single greatest challenge so easily, and continue to grip the club 'neutrally.'

Left-to-right curvature on most shots proves that, by aligning your hands 'neutrally' on the club, you tend to deliver its face at impact **looking to the right of where the clubhead is swinging, or open**. To match the alignment of the clubface to the path of the swing, turn both hands little by little to the right, or into a 'stronger' position, until the curvature is eliminated.* The stronger position of the left hand will have the effect of 'shortening' the thumb position, ie, setting the thumb higher up the shaft.

Right-to-left curvature on most shots proves that, by aligning your hands 'neutrally' on the club, you tend to deliver its face at impact **looking to the left of where the clubhead is swinging, or closed**. The antidote, of course, is the opposite of the above, ie, turning both hands little by little to the left, or into a 'weaker' position, until the curvature is eliminated. The so-called weaker position of the left hand will have the effect of 'lengthening' the thumb position, ie, setting the thumb farther down on the shaft.

Remember, your grip is right *for you* when your shots **fly straight**, even though swing path faults – our next subject – may still push them straight right or pull them straight left of your target.

* To encourage you to persevere with this adjustment, it is worth noting that the weak, short, open-faced, out-to-in, steep-hitting slice that afflicts so many of the world's golfers is, at root, the result of an incorrect grip.

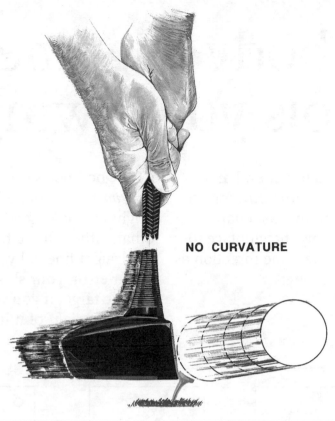

NO CURVATURE

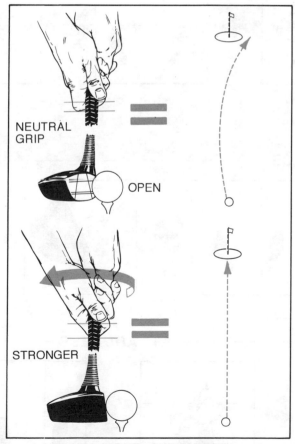

NEUTRAL GRIP

OPEN

STRONGER

LEFT-TO-RIGHT CURVATURE

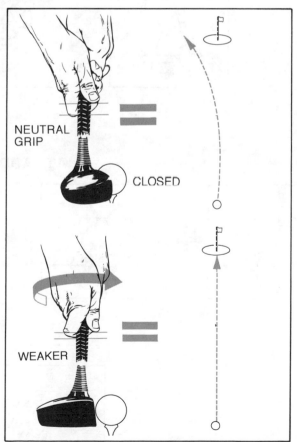

NEUTRAL GRIP

CLOSED

WEAKER

RIGHT-TO-LEFT CURVATURE

CHAPTER 22

Your body alignment controls your swing path

Let's assume that, having found and become comfortable with *your* correct grip, as prescribed in the last chapter, you are now delivering the clubface to the ball looking in the same direction as the clubhead is swinging.

The good news is that you've *eliminated curvature* – stopped your shots slicing right or hooking left. The bad news is that, although the ball is now travelling in a straight line, all you've done is reverse your error: your shots now are pulling *left* of the target if you were slicing, or pushing *right* of it if you were hooking.

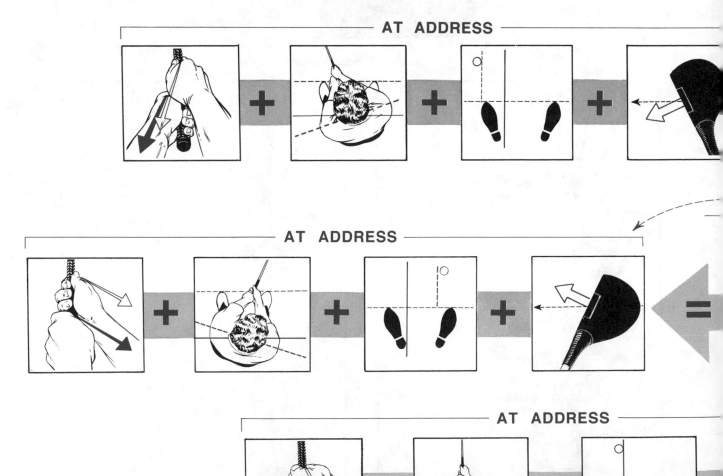

How do you fix that?

Well, let's suppose you'd never read this book, or learned anything elsewhere about golfing cause and effect. What would your *instincts* tell you?

They would tell you that by turning your body around, so that you were aligned **more to the right** if you were a slicer-become-a-puller, or **more to the left** if you were hooker-become-a-pusher, it would become a lot easier to swing the clubhead through impact in the same direction you want the ball to travel, ie, **directly towards your target**, rather than to the left or right of it.

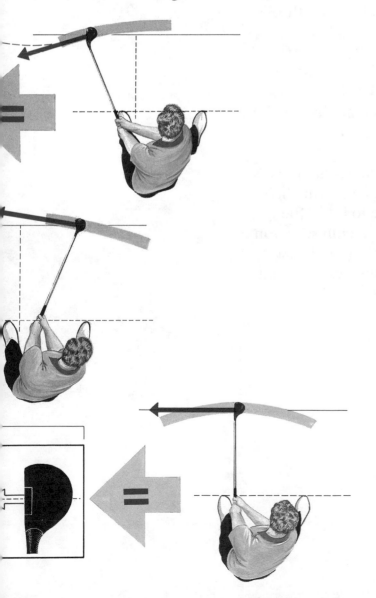

That, as briefly as it can be summarised, is the essence of setting-up to or addressing a golf ball.

If you learn nothing else from this book, imbed the following in your golfing consciousness as deeply as possible:

The grip controls where the clubface looks at impact, which determines the FINAL DIRECTION or CURVATURE of the shot through its inter-action with the path of the clubhead.

The alignment of the body relative to the target line largely controls the direction in which the clubhead is swung through the ball, which determines the STARTING DIRECTION of the shot – *and, if there is no curvature, also its* FINAL DIRECTION.

If you've watched professionals on the practice tee at tournaments, you may have wondered why they spend so much time and effort checking their alignments at address – more, in many cases, than working on actual swing moves.

The above is the answer.

Good golfers are good golfers largely because they have learned and *accepted* that, no matter how fine the gun's firing action, unless it is aimed correctly it won't deliver the missile to the target. Lesser golfers are so impatient to pull the trigger, or so wrapped up in the mechanics of the swing, that they never master what must come before.

Let's encourage you to do so by setting out the necessary steps as clearly as possible.

CHAPTER 23

Select your target, 'see' your target line

Good shot-making begins before a club is even drawn from the bag with clear identification of the target, followed by strong visualisation of a line running from that point straight back to and through the ball.

You will identify your target and 'see' your target line most easily and clearly when standing **directly behind the ball**, rather than sideways on to it.

At this point in their targeting process, better golfers like to picture the flight of the shot they propose to hit in their mind's-eye, as an aid to club selection and as a mental rehearsal of the swing required to produce the desired flight.

CHAPTER 24

Aim the clubface first

With your hands assembling *your* correct grip on the club, and your eyes reaffirming the target line by swivelling from the ball to the target and back a couple of times, move from behind the ball to its side.

With your body and feet still half open to the target, **place the face of the club behind the ball** *so that its bottom edge is exactly at right angles to the target*.

It is imperative that you set the clubface squarely behind the ball before you do anything else, first so that you can **aim yourself** relative to it, and second to ensure that the **ball is correctly positioned** relative to your feet (see Chapter 26).

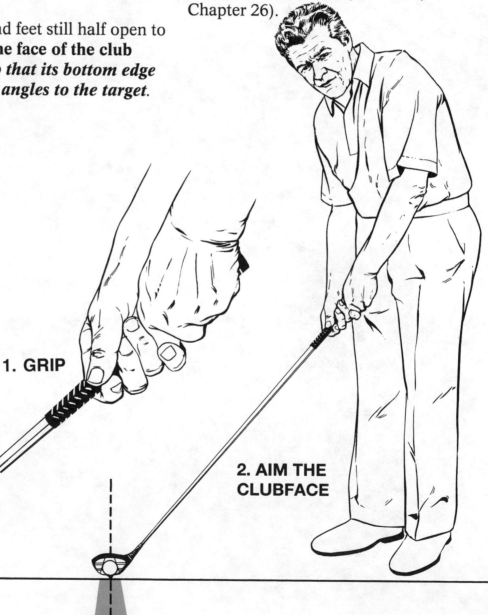

1. GRIP

2. AIM THE CLUBFACE

If you've played golf for a while without undergoing any on-course instruction, it's almost certain that the first things you presently position are your feet, plonking them down in what you hope are the right locations, followed by the clubhead. Break that habit as fast as you can.

Because you must align everything else relative to where it faces, **always – repeat, always – grip and aim the clubhead first**.

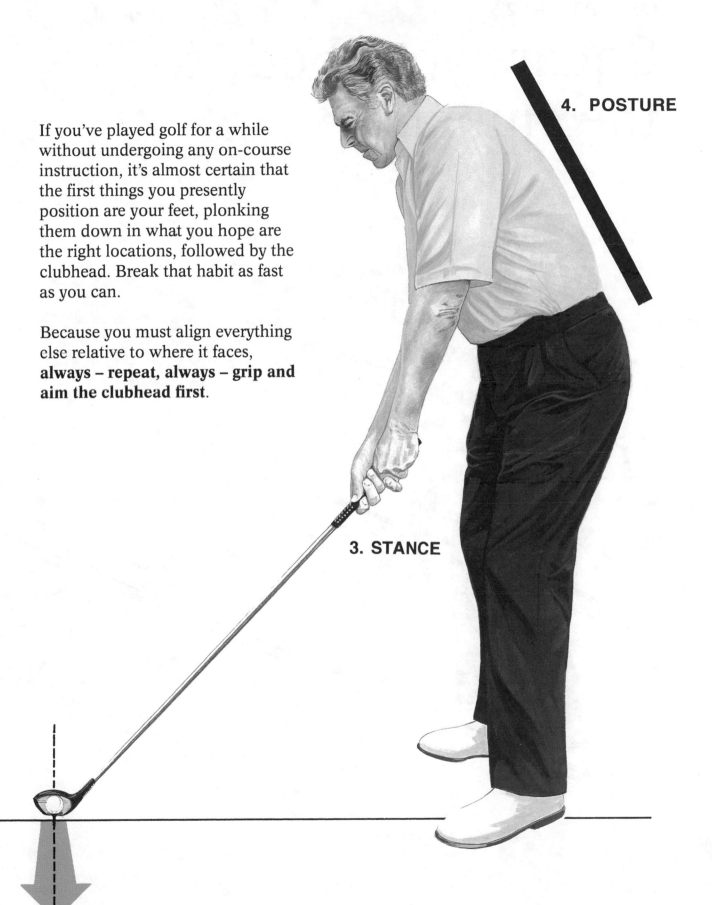

4. POSTURE

3. STANCE

CHAPTER 25

Square your body to the clubface

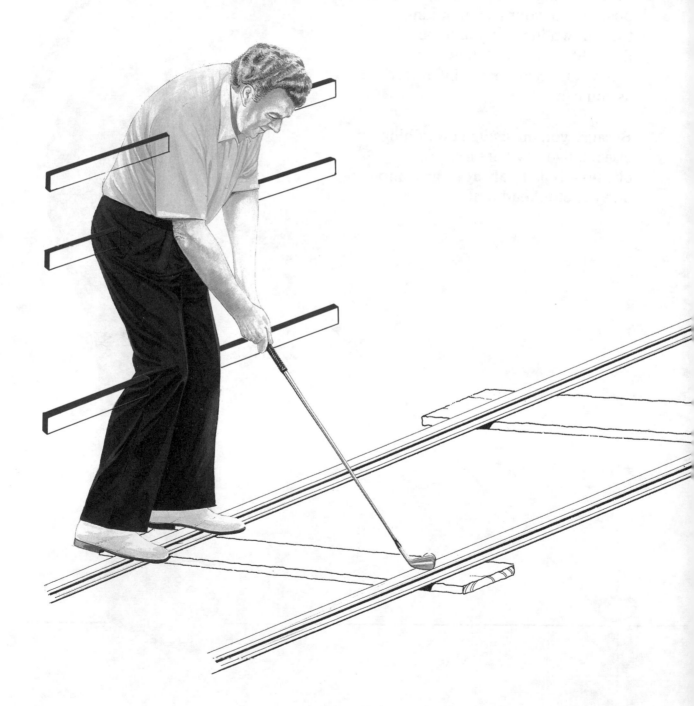

With the clubface set squarely behind the ball, continue moving into position until your body is at **90 degrees** – **ie, square – to its facing**, which means that you will have positioned yourself **parallel to your target line**.

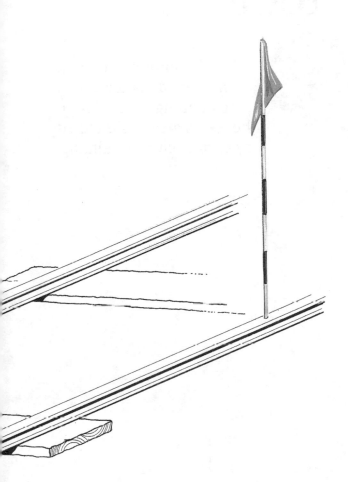

Try to align yourself so that **all parts of you** – your feet, your knees, your hips and your shoulders – are square to the clubface or parallel to the target line (use whichever of these designations you 'see' the best in your mind's-eye).

If setting every part of you square is too uncomfortable at first, work hardest at **aligning your SHOULDERS parallel to your target line**, and worry least about how your feet are positioned.

Because they can see their foot alignment but not how their upper bodies are aimed at address, many golfers find it easy to stand square but hard to align their shoulders parallel to the target line consistently. If you're one such, try 'seeing' your target line as the far rail of a straight piece of railway track, with yourself standing on and matching your shoulder alignment to the near rail.

Another way to check your body alignment is by 'reading' the first part of the ball's flight when you hit practice shots, before sidespin affects its direction. Given solid understanding of golf's impact 'geometry,' shots consistently starting left tell you that you are probably aligned too much that way, or are too 'open,' at address. Conversely, shots starting right indicate that you are aligned too far right, or are too 'closed', at address.

Study the top tournament professionals and you will see them constantly working with teachers or friends on their address angles.

The reason is, of course, that **a gun aimed incorrectly never hits the target.**

CHAPTER 26

Let the aim of the clubface position the ball relative to the feet

The important and often neglected matter of ball positioning in relation to the feet is greatly simplified by correct clubface aiming.

Step up from behind the ball looking down your target line and set the clubface behind the ball. Looking squarely at your target you will notice that, by positioning the face of the club in this way, you also establish a particular alignment of its shaft, and thus also of its handle. It is important when positioning the clubface that the correct loft is maintained.

Now, **without changing that shaft and handle alignment**, finalise your grip on the club and shuffle your feet into what feels like the best position to enable you to hit the ball straight to your target.

'Stand to the club' correctly in this manner and you will find that the ball is automatically positioned correctly in relation to your feet with every club in the bag, including even the putter.

Too simple? Well, give it a try. Particularly if you're one of the many golfers who habitually position their feet before they aim the clubface, you'll be delighted with the results.

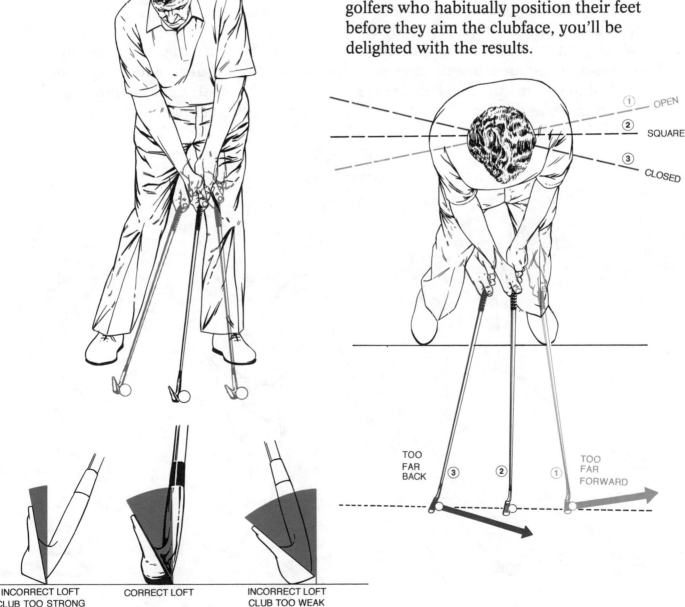

① OPEN
② SQUARE
③ CLOSED

TOO FAR BACK ③ ② ① TOO FAR FORWARD

INCORRECT LOFT CLUB TOO STRONG   CORRECT LOFT   INCORRECT LOFT CLUB TOO WEAK

CHAPTER 27

Check your posture

Correct posture promotes a body pivot that swings the club on the proper in-to-in arc and in the proper plane, which is the only way to return the clubface to the ball squarely and at the correct angle of attack while completely 'releasing' the clubhead.

Grip the club, aim its face, align your body and position the ball correctly and you will automatically achieve most of the postural requirements of a fine set-up. Just to be sure, though, here are the important areas to check:

- To make room for your arms to swing freely past your body, you must **lean over** to the ball. Do so from your **hips**, keeping your back as **straight** as you comfortably can.

- Think **'head up'** rather than 'head down' and achieve it by keeping your chin high.

- Let your arms **hang** easily straight down from your shoulders, keeping your left arm **straight** but not stiff and your right arm **relaxed** at the elbow.

- Because your right hand is lower on the club than your left, your shoulders will **tilt** slightly to the **right**, which will encourage positioning of your head **behind** the ball. Go with the tendency but don't exaggerate it.

- Stay well **balanced** and **'springy'** by setting your weight **equally** between the balls of both feet, with your knees slightly **flexed**.

CHAPTER 28
The slice-producing chain-reaction

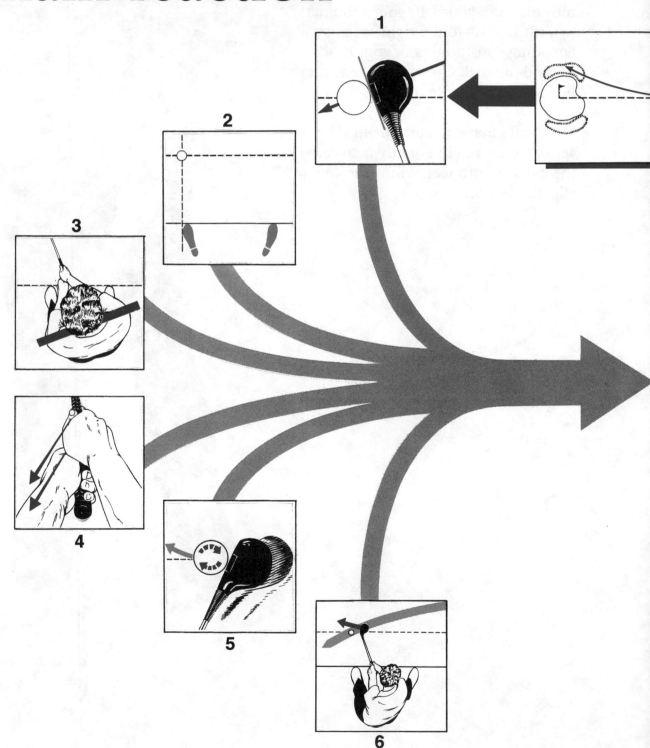

The importance for all golfers of aiming the gun correctly before pulling the trigger cannot be over-stated. To dramatise it, we'll end this section with another look at the chain-reactions of faults that frustrate so many people who set about the game with insufficient understanding of, or attention to, its laws of cause and effect.

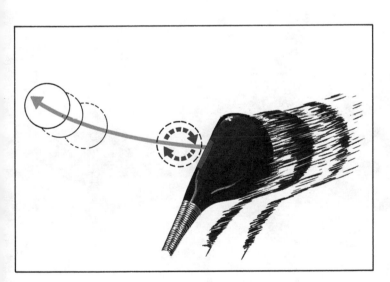

Because so many golfers slice so many of their long shots, here, first, is the chain-reaction most often underlying that affliction:

• The ball continually finishes **right** of target.

• In an instinctive effort to stop that, the clubface at address is aimed **left** of target. (1)

•Aiming the clubface left causes the ball to be positioned too far **forward** in the stance. (2)

• Addressing the ball so far forward pulls the shoulders **open** – aligns them **left** of the target (even though the feet may be set square to the target line). (3)

• The open-shouldered alignment forces the hands to grip too '**weakly**' – to be positioned too much on top of the club or towards the target. (4)

• The weak grip prevents the clubface from being squared at impact, delivering it to the ball looking **right** of target or **open**. (5)

• The too-far forward ball position and open shoulders force delivery of the clubhead to the ball from **outside to in** across the target line, and at an excessively steep angle of approach. (6)

• Struck with an oblique cutting-across action, the ball **starts** to the **left** of target but then **spins** weakly to the **right**.

And, of course, the more such a golfer follows his instincts, the more surely the ball will slice.

CHAPTER 29

The hook-producing chain-reaction

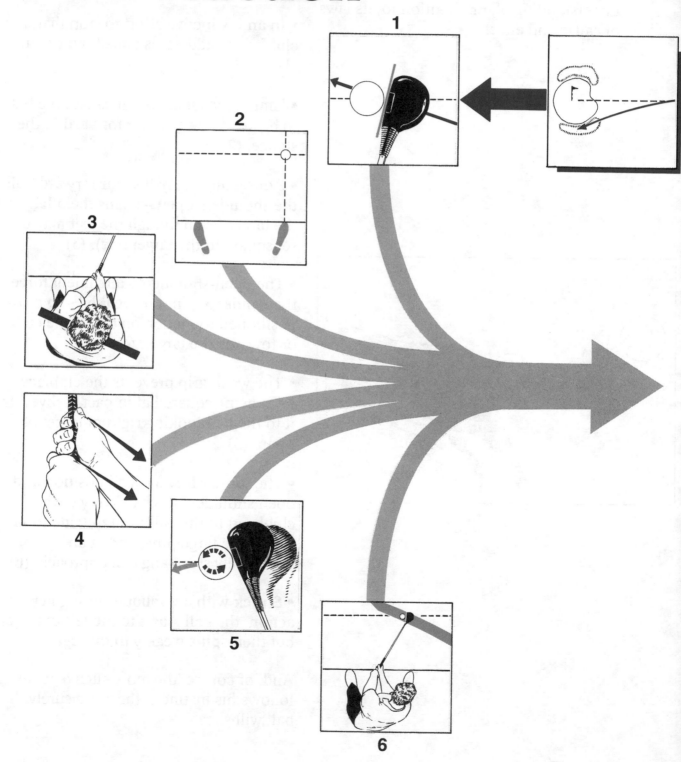

Here's the chain-reaction resulting from instinctive rather than cause-and-effect-based curative measures when a golfer's innate tendency is to hook most of the longer shots:

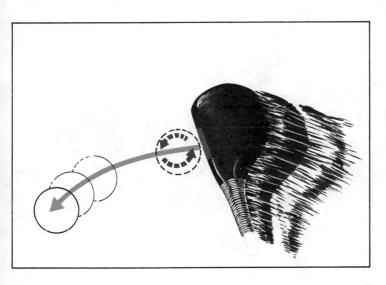

• The ball continually finishes **left** of target.

• In an instinctive effort to stop that, the clubface at address is aimed **right** of target. (1)

• Aiming the clubface right causes the ball to be positioned too far **back** in the stance. (2)

• Addressing the ball so far back pulls the shoulders **closed** – aligns them **right** of the target (even though the feet may be set square to the target line). (3)

• The closed-shoulder alignment forces the hands to grip too '**strongly**' – to be positioned too much to the right or away from the target. (4)

• The strong grip delivers the clubface looking to the left of the target or **closed**. (5)

• The rearward ball position and closed shoulders force delivery of the clubhead to the ball from **inside to out** across the target line, and sometimes at so low an angle of approach that the ground is contacted before the ball. (6)

• Struck with an oblique drawing-across action, the ball starts to the **right** of the target but then spins strongly to the **left**.

And, of course, the more such a golfer follows his instincts, the more surely – and usually the further – the ball will hook.

CHAPTER 30
The chain-reaction of great golf

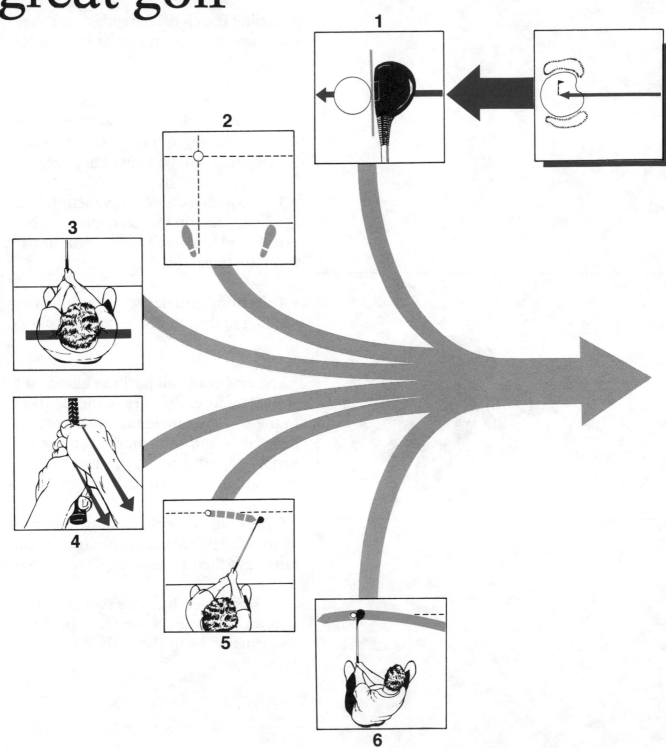

Here's the chain-reaction of the player who, first, understands the 'geometry' of golf, then always prepares for his shots in accordance with its laws of cause and effect:

• The ball more often than not **starts** along and **continues** on the **target line** all the way to the target.

• Straight flight promotes aiming the clubface at address **squarely** at the target.

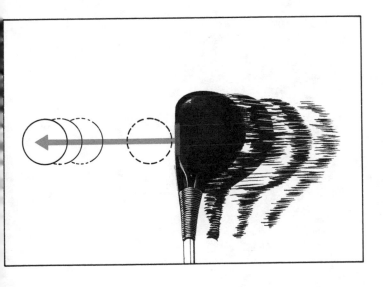

• Squaring the clubface to the target promotes proper ball positioning.

• Correct ball positioning promotes correct body aiming, ie, shoulder and hip alignment.

• All of the above help maintain the correct grip.

• Struck with the clubhead travelling momentarily **directly along** rather than across the target line, and at an approach angle producing **flush** back-of-ball contact, the ball starts and continues **straight to the target**.

I hope the fact that only now, more than halfway through this book, are we ready to begin looking at swing technique will convince you of the importance of understanding exactly what you are trying to do with the business end of your golf clubs each time you pull them from the bag, and of how major a bearing your *preparation* for each swing will have on its outcome.

Understand and remember above all else how the things you do at address determine how the club impacts the ball, with these priorities:

1 • **GRIP for correct clubface alignment.**

2 • **Clubface AIM and body alignment.**

3 • **STANCE for correct swing direction.**

4 • **POSTURE for correct swing plane and complete clubhead 'release'.**

PART FOUR

The swing

CHAPTER 31
Keeping it simple

You are now taking great care to, pre-programme, as far as possible, correct impact through your grip, clubface aim, ball position, and body alignment and posture.

All that remains for you to play the best golf of which you are capable is to swing the club on a plane and in a direction that transmits your address 'geometry' to the ball, while also generating sufficient clubhead speed to propel it the required distance.

How do you do that?

Because the ball is lying on the ground to the side of you, the answer is with an **upward and downward swinging of the arms combined with a rotational motion of the body**.

How much arm swinging relative to how much body rotation? How 'steeply' up and down should your arms swing relative to the 'aroundness" of your body motion? Which drives what – the arm swinging the body rotation, or the body rotation the arm swinging? Where does the power come from – the swinging of the arms or the rotating of the body?

All those questions, and all others like them, will quickly become moot if you will simply do as follows:

Swing your left arm directly back from the ball, allowing it to move progressively upward and backward – ie, to the inside of the target line – as a natural response to the rotation of your shoulders around the axis of your spine.

Can the golf swing really be *that* simple?

Because so many golfers believe they will play better by understanding what they are trying to do with the club move by move, we'll talk a little more about the mechanics of the action in the following chapters. However, if you ever reach the point of feeling that your chief golfing problem has become 'paralysis by analysis,' **forgetting everything but the above concept of backswing motion** might delightfully surprise you.

To grasp it better, study the illustration here of a golfer swinging beneath a sheet of glass inclined so that it matches his left-arm angle at address, with a hinged segment containing a hole cut out for his head.

Note how the club remains constantly 'in plane,' while also swinging in the correct direction relative to the target line, **so long as the golfer's backward- and upward-swinging left arm constantly brushes the large area of glass, while his shoulders follow the angle of inclination of the smaller segment.**

Swing back like this and golf will be easier than you ever imagined possible.

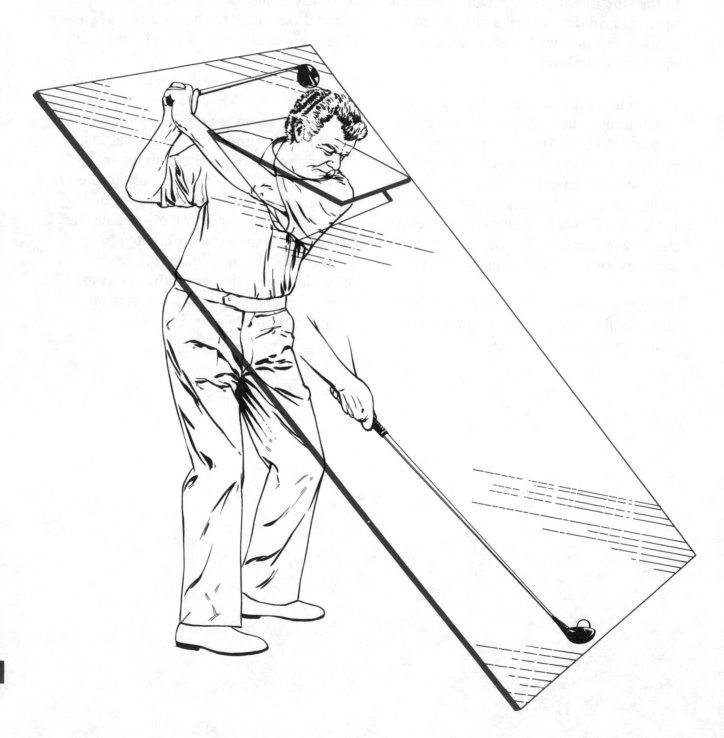

CHAPTER 32

Shoulders turn flatter than arms swing

As we repeat the drawing of the golfer swinging under glass from a slightly different angle, note again how his **shouders rotate on a shallower or 'flatter' plane than the plane of his arm swing.**

Contrary to what you may have heard or read, this separation of planes happens in the swings of most good golfers, and in the swings of *all* great golfers. The reason lies in achieving the correct proportion of body movement relative to the action of the arms in the downswing.

Only by freely swinging his arms **past**, not *with*, his body can a golfer deliver to the ball all of the centrifugal force generated in the head of the club, while at the same time re-squaring its face to the target.

To whatever extent either his shoulders or arms move too much 'around' or excessively 'up and down' relative to each other, **speed will be lost and the alignment of the clubface and the path of the clubhead distorted at impact.**

CHAPTER 33

'Over the top' and 'rock and block'

For the first half of the nearly 50 years I have taught golf, swinging the arms too shallowly or flatly – locking them too closely or tightly to the torso – was by far the most prevalent fault among players seeking my help.

Since then, swinging the arms on too straight or steep a path, mostly as a result of rocking or tilting rather than rotating or pivoting the shoulders, has increasingly become the most persistent

mistake, particularly among fairly capable golfers seeking to raise their games to the next level.

When the shoulders rotate on the correct plane but the arms swing insufficiently upward – ie, shoulders brushing the hinged glass panel but arms swinging BELOW the main sheet – the arms become too tightly 'married' to the body to be able to swing freely **past** it in the downswing.

The result is an involuntary effort to make up for what the arms, wrists and hands should be doing, **but physically can't**, with premature and usually excessive body action – the ugly and sadly destructive 'over the top' move so much in evidence each weekend on golf courses all around the world.

When the opposite 'bad marriage' occurs, that is shoulders tilting or rocking rather than rotating, forcing the arms to swing predominantly upward rather than **upward and INWARD** – ie, both shoulders and arms *breaking through* the glass panels – the reciprocal tilting or rocking of the shoulders in the downswing prevents the body from unwinding freely, thereby again inhibiting the arms from swinging freely **past** it.

The result in this case is that the arms slow down prematurely, forcing the wrists either to lock and push or push-slice the ball to the right off an open clubface, or unhinge independently, pulling or pull-hooking the shot to the left off a closed clubface. Or, as I like to call it, the 'rock and block' so much in evidence on the American tour in the 1960s and 1970s, concurrent with Jack Nicklaus's huge success employing a straighter or steeper or more upright action of both the arms and shoulders than most of his predecessors.

So remember:

To be able to swing the club FREELY DOWN AND PAST YOUR BODY, rather than 'with' your body or with your body 'in your way,' you must first swing the club UP and it will come IN as your shoulders ROTATE.

CHAPTER 34

'Uprightness' and 'flatness': the realities

If you are already a fairly experienced or able golfer, I'm sure you will still want to ask: 'How "upright" or "flat" will following these instructions make me?'

The answer is that, unless you **manipulate** your arms and/or shoulders **out of plane** at some point during the swing by, if you will, shoving them through or dropping them below the sheet of glass, the overall 'shape' or 'look' of the action will be **determined entirely by your build and the length of the club you are using**.

If you are tall, you will naturally stand relatively **close** to the ball, which will naturally produce relatively **steep** angles of arm and body inclination at address, which will, in turn, naturally produce a relatively **'upright'** arm plane combined with a **somewhat tilted** shoulder turn. Also, of course, the shorter the shaft of the club you are using, requiring you to stand even closer to the ball, the steeper or more 'upright' everything will naturally become.

If you are short, the reverse will naturally occur, ie, you will naturally stand **farther** from the ball at address, thus will naturally have **shallower** angles of arm and body inclination, and thus will naturally swing on a relatively **'flat'** arm plane combined with a less tilted or more nearly **horizontal** turn of the

shoulders. And, of course, the longer the shaft of the club being used, the shallower or 'flatter' both planes will naturally become.

Please note the repeated use of the word **naturally** in those last two paragraphs.

Given only that you have gripped properly then aimed, aligned and arranged your body correctly at the ball, swinging naturally is by far the easiest way to swing both in plane and in the correct direction with every club in the bag.

CHAPTER 35

Swinging in the proper direction

Seen from behind you looking down your target line, the shaft of the club at the top of your backswing can be aligned in one of only three directions.

You can swing the club to the position known in golfing lingo as 'laid off', meaning that it's aligned to the left of your target line. You can swing so that the club 'crosses the line', meaning it's aligned to the right of your target. Or you can swing so that you complete the backswing 'on line', meaning that the shaft line matches or parallels your target line.

Assuming you want to hit the ball straight to the target, you will do so most easily **by reaching the 'on line' position at the completion of the backswing**. Here's why.

The downswing, when performed at its best, is **reaction** rather than a consciously-controlled action. That being the case, how you swing down will largely be governed by how you swung back.

Thus, when the shaft of the club and the target line 'match' at the completion of the backswing, **the club is ideally positioned or 'aimed' to swing down and through the ball travelling momentarily directly along the target line**.

ON LINE

IN TO SQUARE TO IN

In the same manner, when the club is laid off at the top, its reciprocal path through impact is likely to be across the line from **out to in**, resulting in either a pull or a fade/slice depending on where the clubface looks. And, of course, when the shaft crosses the line at the top, its reciprocal path is likely to be across the line from **in to out**, resulting in either a push or a draw/hook depending on the clubface alignment.

I used the phrase 'ideally positioned' a moment ago regarding matched shaft and target lines at the top of the swing because of the part the grip plays in keeping them matched through impact.

When a player habitually misses his target due to an incorrect clubface alignment at impact, he'll often attempt to redirect the swing coming down, either to the outside if his shots are finishing right or to the inside if they are finishing left. Thus the **expectancy** of straight shots created by correct gripping

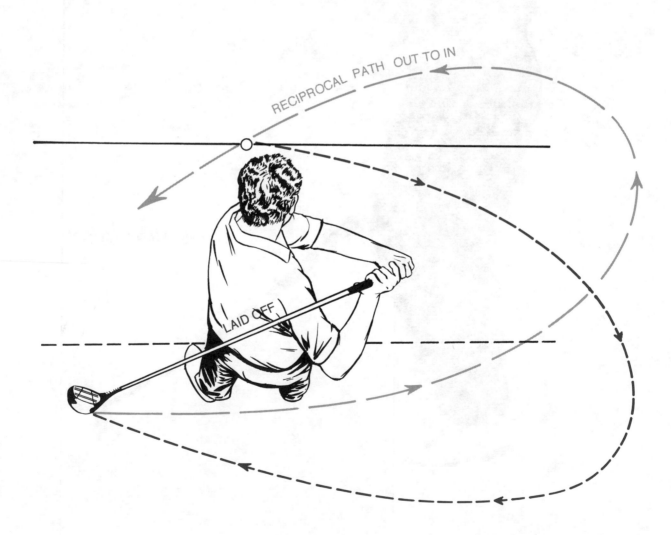

RECIPROCAL PATH OUT TO IN

LAID OFF

is an important factor in reciprocating one's backswing 'geometry' during the downswing.

How else do you keep your swing 'on line'?

I cannot overstate that you will have great trouble doing so with any consistency unless you begin the swing from an **on-line set up**. In other words, the best way to ensure an on-line swing at impact is to grip and aim the club and align and arrange the body correctly at address. Or, yet again, back to basics.

It's really this simple:

If from a correct set up you achieve the proper balance between 'aroundness' of body rotation and 'upwardness' of arm motion, **by concentrating on swinging in plane**, you will automatically also swing in the **proper direction**. So set up correctly and swing to the set-up, avoiding any re-routing of the swing path.

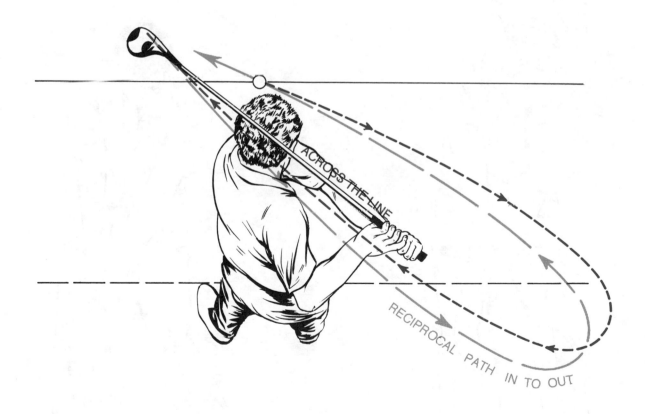

ACROSS THE LINE

RECIPROCAL PATH IN TO OUT

CHAPTER 36

Rhythm and tempo

Jerking and rushing the club back are among the most common faults I encounter at every level of golf short of the very top. Their most common causes are anxiety and confusion regarding swing technique, producing an almost irresistible urge to get the action over with as fast as possible. On the physical level, the great destroyer is excessive muscular tension, particularly when it 'freezes' the player into total immobility at address.

Understanding exactly what you are trying to do when you swing, then consciously trying to do it, conditions your mind to allow you to begin the action at a leisurely pace and with a fluidity of motion.

Remaining slightly in motion in some part of your body throughout your set-up procedure, then initiating the swing with a confidence-building 'trigger', guards your muscles against locking up.

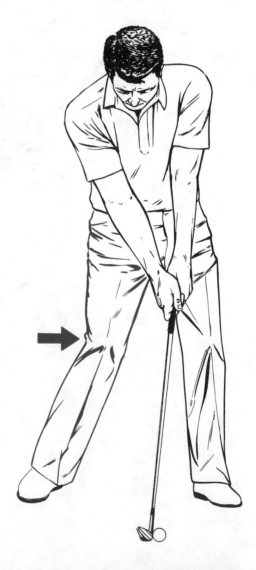

Stay relaxed over the ball by gently **easing your legs and shoulders** and **'hanging' your arms loosely** as you complete your set up. Watch good players to get a feel for these tiny but vital tension-fighters.

There are numerous ways to trigger the swing, from Sam Snead's and Jack Nicklaus's famous chin-swivel to Gary Player's pronounced right knee kick-in.

Most effective for most people is the **forward-press**: a slight targetwards inclination of the hands and hips from which the player, so to speak, 'rebounds' into a running start.

Again, study the triggers of good players, experiment to find the one that works best for you, then practise it until it becomes second nature.

CHAPTER 37

The backswing

The most easy and consistent way to start and continue the backswing on the plane and in the direction dictated by your set up, is simply to **retain your address posture while swinging the club away from the ball without any moving part of you working independently of any other part**.

To meet the postural requirement, focus on retaining your **knee flex** and **angle of spinal inclination** while keeping your head reasonably steady. Unless you want to prevent your shoulders from rotating correctly, never even think of keeping your head 'down,' let alone attempt to do so.

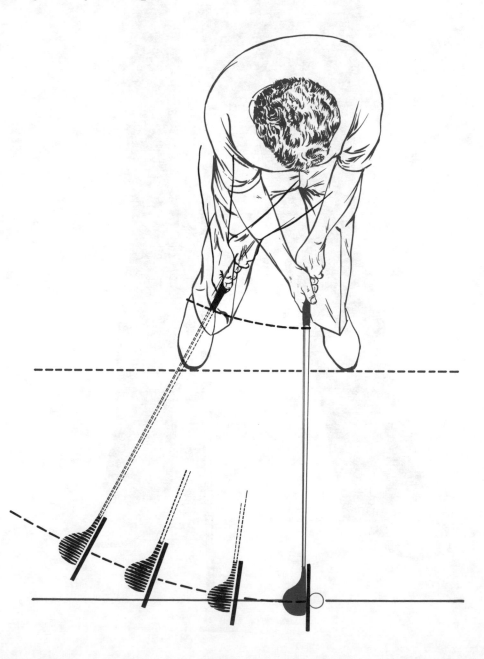

Visualising the club shaft as a continuation of your easily-extended left arm will help you to start back smoothly and cohesively, as will feeling that your entire left side from the head of the club to your shoulder moves back from the ball **as a single unit**. Avoiding any sense of lifting, twisting, or other form of manipulation of the club with your hands, wrists, or arms **independently of your upper-body rotation** will also be helpful.

Your swing plane and direction are correct when the clubhead moves to the **inside** of the target line; when its path

relative to the ground remains **shallow**; and when its face stays square (ie, at 90 degrees) to the arc it is describing.

As the action progresses, let your easily-extended left arm follow its natural inclination to rotate a little, thereby allowing the club to swing **back** to the **inside** as well as **up**, but **never independent** of your rotating shoulders.

Allow your wrists to hinge or cock as a natural and gradual response to the **momentum of the rising clubhead** – never by 'working' them independently of your other motions.

Keep your left arm easily extended all the way to the completion of the backswing, to ensure the **width of arc** necessary to produce the proper angle of attack at impact.

Above all, from your first movement to the point where you begin to change direction, seek a sense that your arm swing and shoulder rotation are **totally in sync** – that neither at any point gets ahead of or behind the other.

CHAPTER 38

The downswing

Grip correctly, set up correctly, swing the club back on the correct plane and in the correct direction – that is, with your arms flowing up and back as your shoulders rotate against the resistance of your lower body – and you've done just about everything you consciously can to hit a fine golf shot.

The reason is that the downswing happens too fast to be consciously

controlled move by move. Which means, of course, that it occurs at its best as a pure **reflex action** to whatever has gone before. Which explains why – particularly when practising your technique – you must go to such great pains to get everything right, as in setting up the shot and swinging the club back correctly.

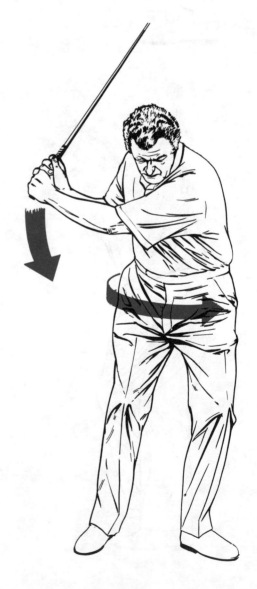

If you feel a need to have some sort of downswing concept when trying to score on the course, focus on coordinating the downward motion of your hands and arms with the uncoiling motions of your legs and hips, thereby ensuring that you square the clubface to the ball at optimum speed by swinging your arms freely **past**, rather than *with*, your body.

The desired feel is one of hitting the ball to the target rather than swinging the club to the ball.

Remember that shots starting and continuing straight left, or starting left and curving right, indicate that your legs and hips are out-racing your arm swing and wrist action. Conversely shots

starting and continuing straight right, or starting right and curving left, indicate the opposite – that your arm swing and wrist action are out-racing your lower body clearance.

Get the elements over which you have conscious control right: grip, aim, set-up and backswing – and all your

reactions will promote *correctness in the final element, the actual striking of the ball.*

Difficult as we all find that at times, it's by far the simplest way to play the game of golf.

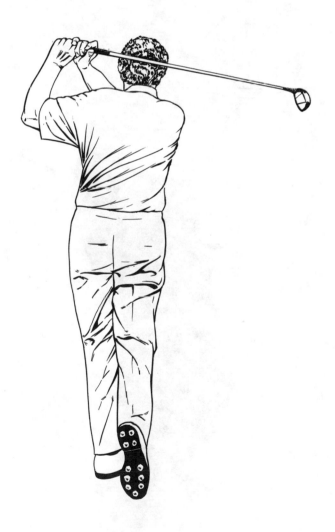

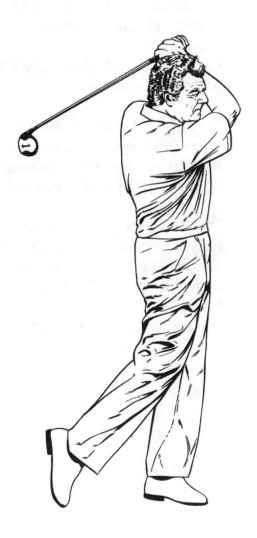

CHAPTER 39

Distance is clubhead speed *correctly applied*

Let me remind you yet again that 'correctly applied' means:

• Clubface square to target at impact;

• Clubhead path momentarily coinciding with target line at impact;

• Angle of attack appropriate to club being used at impact.

Never forget that, *no matter how high your clubhead speed*, the greater the error in any one of those angles the less USEFUL DISTANCE you will gain.

That being the case, in positioning the body to provide an adequate amount of clubhead speed at impact, the backswing must still set the club in the plane and direction that offer the best chance of also achieving correct impact.

In both respects I would like you to visualise yourself as a giant coil spring at work.

Your **torso** from your shoulders to your waist comprises the upper portion of the spring, stabilized in space by your **steady head**. Your **hips and legs** form the lower portion of the spring, firmly anchored by your **solidly planted feet**.

Now relate the coiling action of the spring to your swinging motions.

As you swing the club progressively farther back and up, the top portion of the spring, or your **upper half**, coils progressively tighter and tighter against the resistance of the spring's bottom portion, or your **lower half**.

The less motion you permit below your waist relative to the amount your torso rotates above it, the tighter you will coil the spring. The tighter you coil the spring – **given also correct impact** – the farther you will hit the ball.

CHAPTER 40

Your personal power potential

How powerful a golfer can *you* as an individual expect to be?

The answer depends on your physique, your level of conditioning, your hand-eye coordination, your capacity for working at golf, and what it is about the game that most turns you on.

At the top end of the power scale are the young, strong, limber, finely-coordinated, practise-and-play-every-day golfers – ie, tour professionals and top amateurs – who can rotate their upper bodies through many degrees with minimal motion in their lower halves, **while still positioning the club for correct impact**. By so doing they generate tremendous torque that is converted by centrifugal force into very high clubhead speed at impact, thereby producing those prodigious drives we all envy so much.

From there on down, the power scale consists of less well-conditioned, or less flexible, or not so finely coordinated, or older, or play-but-never-practise types – the great mass of recreational golfers, in other words. To be able to swing their arms sufficiently up and turn their shoulders sufficiently around to **position**

the club for correct impact, the vast majority of these players must settle for a looser winding of the spring by allowing their legs to work more freely and their hips to rotate more fully and easily in response to their upper-body rotation.

Experience is really the only way to discover where you fall on this scale, as gained over time both on the practice tee and the golf course itself. Where you come out will depend greatly on what it is about golf that gives you the greatest satisfaction.

If the game to you is largely a test of *machismo* – belting the drive out beyond all your pals, getting home with the shortest possible iron – your focus will surely be fixed on raw clubhead speed, no matter how frustrating your endless wild shots become.

If you are the type of person to whom the game is more about scoring and winning, then correct application will quickly become and remain your top priority.

And if you want to be a champion golfer?

Then, of course, you present yourself with the game's single biggest and most eternal challenge: finding and then maintaining the perfect balance between generating clubhead speed and delivering it correctly.

PART FIVE

Answers to most-asked questions

CHAPTER 41
'Timing'

Q I constantly encounter references to 'timing', but never a clear explanation of it. What *is* 'timing'?

A Expressed as simply as possible, the golf swing, to use one of my favourite teaching phrases, consists of **'two turns and a swish'**: that is, a rotational coiling and uncoiling of the body combined with an up-and-down swinging of the hands, arms and club, as both units are supported by the feet and legs.

When the pace and rhythm of the hand and arm action so synchronise with the body action that the club impacts the ball **squarely and at optimum speed**, the swing and/or the shot is said to have been perfectly 'timed.'

What that really means, of course, in non-golfing language, is that the 'turns' and the 'swish' have been perfectly **coordinated**.

Attempting to coordinate their 'turns' and 'swish' perfectly is the chief reason tournament professionals practise so much, and their ability to do so is the factor most separating them from handicap players.

Here's how to identify and fix the two chief 'timing' problems you'll encounter, assuming that your grip, set-up, and swing mechanics are sound:

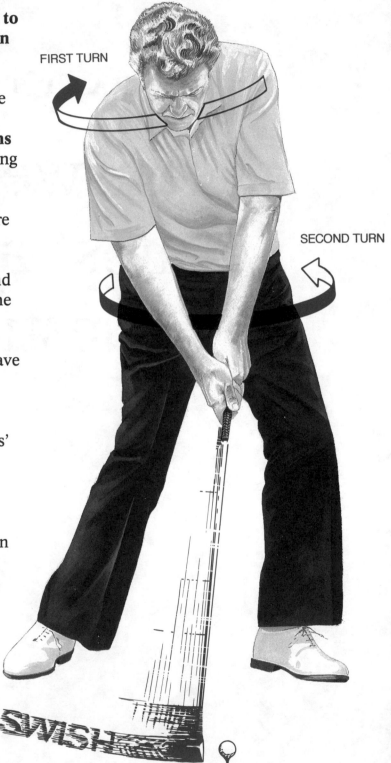

FIRST TURN

SECOND TURN

SWISH

Shots sliced, topped to the left, or 'thinned'

CAUSE: your body is unwinding faster than your hands and arms are swinging the club down, thus preventing the radius formed by your left arm and club shaft at address from being fully restored at impact. This excessively 'late' hit leaves the clubface open, hence the slice, or delivers the bottom of the clubhead to the upper part of the ball in the case of the topped and 'thinned' shots.

CURE: be sure that you have not 'weakened' your grip or are opening your shoulders at address. Then deliver the clubhead 'in time' by focusing on swinging your hands and arms down from the top of the backswing, which will automatically slow your body rotation. Apply this medicine on the 'soft' shots as well as those calling for full power.

Shots hooked, topped to the right, or hit heavy or 'fat'

CAUSE: you are 'restoring the radius' too soon by swinging your hands and arms down faster than your body is unwinding, causing the clubhead to have closed if it reaches the ball cleanly (draw or hook), or to be travelling upward by the time it reaches the ball (top), or to contact the ground before arriving at the ball (heavy or 'fat' hit).

CURE: check that you have not 'strengthened' your grip or are misaiming the clubface at address. Then deliver the clubhead 'in time' by focusing on *unwinding* your hips through the ball from the top of the backswing, which will automatically slow down your hand and arm action.

CHAPTER 42

The head

Q 'Keep your head down,' says my partner every time I miss a shot. 'Keep your head still,' say most top players and teachers. Is this as important as everyone makes out?

A 'Keep your head down and you'll keep me in business forever' has been another of my favourite sayings through all the years I've been teaching golf.

The reason is that keeping the head **down**, to the point where the chin sits on or close to the chest, forces a tilting rather than a rotating or coiling action of the shoulders in the backswing, leading to all manner of other ugly moves – and even uglier shots.

Trying to keep the head **still** is better than attempting to keep it down – just as

long as doing so doesn't inhibit free and fluid upward and downward swinging of the hands and arms or rotation of the body away from and then towards the target.

For most golfers, the best thought is to keep the head **steady** enough to permit both of the above actions with the least possible change in the axis of the body, as represented by the upper part of the spine, during its coiling and uncoiling.

Swivelling the chin away from the target just before or as you start back, in the manner of Sam Snead or Jack Nicklaus and many other top golfers, promotes freedom and fluidity of motion while keeping the axis steady.

CHAPTER 43

The arms

Q   What role do the arms play in the golf swing relative to other parts of the body?

A The arms must be swung freely to play good golf, but never to the point where their motion gets out of sync with the coiling of the body in the backswing and its uncoiling in the downswing.

As I have explained and reiterated many times in this book, during the backswing the arms swing **up** as the body rotates away from the target, then during the downswing the arms swing **down** as the body rotates towards the target.

Some good golfers feel that their bodies coil in response to the swinging of their

arms, while others feel that their arm swinging is generated by the coiling of the body. Either feeling is fine, just so long as it produces **complete coordination** of the two actions – that is, does not cause one to lag behind or get ahead of the other at any point in the swing.

To witness how freely the arms of a really fine golfer swing the club to the ball, stand facing him and watch the space between his hands and right shoulder during the downswing. You will hardly believe how fast it widens.

Now watch that friend of yours with the large handicap and the even larger slice. Because he spins his whole upper body mass into the shot before he swings his arms downward, the space opens much more slowly.

The single best way to learn and ingrain free and fluid arm swinging is by **hitting shots with your feet together** – and I mean *really* together, with the heels touching. You'll have become a fine arm swinger when you can hit the ball within 20 yards of your normal distance while remaining totally in balance.

CHAPTER 44
The legs and hips

Q How much should I use my legs and hips, and what should they do?

A During the backswing you should use your legs and hips to resist the rotation of your upper body, but *only to the degree* that you are still able to set the club at the top on a plane and in a direction that produces **correct impact**.

Get the balance right and your leg and hip action during the downswing will, more often than not, happen correctly and automatically. That's because setting the club correctly at the top promotes delivering it to the ball from inside to straight along the target line, which in turn promotes clearing the left side to make room for the hands and arms to swing through correctly.

Highly skilled golfers are able to restrict their lower-half backswing motion to, at most, a slight raising of the left heel, a pulling of the left knee inward toward a still-flexed right knee, and a tugging of the hips through about half as much rotation as the shoulders, while still positioning the club for correct impact.

Less gifted players usually cannot swing the club on the plane and in the direction that returns it correctly to the ball without 'giving' more in their legs and hips in response to their upward-swinging arms and rotating shoulders. However, there must always be *some* resistance from below the waist, in order for the player to be able to swing the club rather than himself.

The simplest and usually the best 'feels' for producing sound leg action among the majority of golfers are of simultaneously rotating the shoulders and swinging the club up in the backswing, then of rotating the hips as the arms swing the club down and through the ball.

CHAPTER 45

'Out to in'

Q Why do I hit across from out to in on so many shots?

A By far the most probable reason is a chain-reaction of set up errors ingrained since you first took up the game by constantly delivering the clubface looking to the right of its direction of travel, as follows.

• In an instinctive effort to prevent your long shots from finishing to the right, you aim the clubface to the left of your target at address (1).

• The more to the left you aim the clubface, the farther forward in your stance you position the ball (2).

• The farther forward you position the ball, the more left of target you align your shoulders in order to be able to set the club behind the ball at address (3).

• Your forward ball position and open shoulders have the effect of 'weakening' your grip relative to your target line (4).

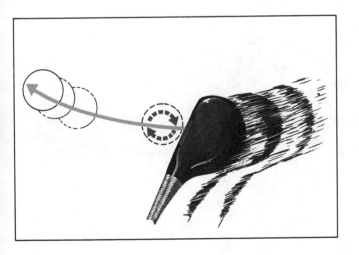

• Prevented by your open shoulders from starting the clubhead back from the ball correctly, you quickly manoeuvre it to the inside of your target line, either by spinning your shoulders or by pulling your arms in that direction, or both – probably while also fanning the clubface open with your hands and forearms (5).

• Reciprocating those backswing moves, you start down by throwing or heaving your entire upper body mass – shoulders, arms, hands, club – over and around towards the target line (6).

• This continuing pattern of movement delivers the clubhead to the ball steeply across the target line from outside to inside.

• The clubface mostly arrives at the ball open to that swing path, producing a slice with the least-lofted clubs and straight-left pulls when the backspin produced by lots of clubface loft nullifies the effect of sidespin.

Sadly, most people who 'play' golf this way are convinced their problem lies in the way they swing the club. The *truth* is that it is caused almost entirely by faulty gripping, clubface aiming, ball positioning, body alignment, and posture.

Learn to set up correctly with the help of the appropriate chapters herein. If you will thereafter concentrate only on swinging your arms 'down' from the top of the backswing, I think you will find golf more enjoyable than you ever believed possible.

CHAPTER 46

'In to out'

Q I'm a pretty good player, but tend to miss a lot of shots by swinging too much from in to out. Why?

A As with the out-to-in swingers, most in-to-outers ingrain a chain-reaction of set-up errors by habitually delivering the clubface looking to the left of its direction of travel, as follows.

• The instinctive reaction when shots go repeatedly left is to try to prevent that by aiming the clubface more and more to the right of the target at address (1).

• The more to the right the clubface is aimed, the farther back in the stance the ball is positioned (2).

• The farther back the ball is positioned, the more right of target the shoulders must be aligned in order to be able to set the club behind the ball at address (3).

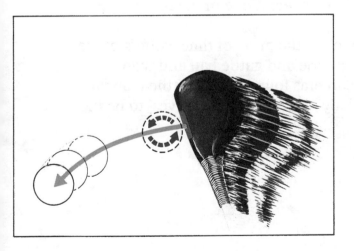

• The rearward ball position along with the closed shoulders have the effect of 'strengthening' the player's grip relative to his target line (4).

• The closed shoulders and strong grip promote swinging the arms up too much to the inside, which causes the shoulders to tilt or rock instead of turning or rotating, with the clubface often tending to roll inward into a closed position (5).

• Reciprocating the backswing moves, the shoulders rock rather than rotate in the downswing, blocking the arms from swinging freely past the body. In combination, those actions cause the wrists to function independently, either rolling the clubface closed through impact and hooking the shot, or holding it open and pushing the shot (6).

As with the out-to-inners, golfers who have ingrained an in-to-out clubhead path as a response to shots constantly finishing left are inclined to look for the solution to their bad shots in a different way of swinging the club. The *truth* once again is that the solution lies mostly in improving their set up to the ball.

First, take the time and trouble to correct your grip, your clubface aim, your ball position, your body alignment, and your posture. Then concentrate during the downswing simply on turning your hips 'out of the way' to allow your arms to swing freely past your body, thus enabling you to hit the ball to the target rather than swing the club to the ball.

CHAPTER 47

'Methods'

Q You read and hear a lot about one top player using this 'method' and another using some other 'method.' Are there really different methods of swinging, and, if so, which is the best?

A Let me first remind you of our opening statement:

'The golf swing has only one purpose: to deliver the head of the club to the ball correctly. How that is done is immaterial, so long as the method used permits correct impact to be achieved over and over and over again.'

Having said that – and while the precise mechanics of the best players' swings do and will forever remain somewhat individualistic – it does seem to me that, over the past decade or two, a greater

consensus has been reached about more areas of golf technique than ever before.

A prime example is the now almost universally accepted importance of the set up in determining how the club is delivered to the ball at impact. Another example is how much the positioning of the ball on the ground relative to the player influences the 'shape' – ie, the plane and the direction – of his swing.

My nearly 50 years of teaching tell me that the concept of 'plane' has long been and remains the most confusing element of swing technique or 'methodology.'

Back in the mists of time, golfers of the featherie and guttie ball and wooden shaft eras found swinging the club fairly 'flatly' or 'around themselves' to be the

most effective way of raising the missile into the air as well as propelling it forward. Then, as the rubber-cored ball and steel shaft promoted shorter and firmer swings, they also gave rise to the notion that swinging straighter – ie, with the clubhead remaining closer to the target line or moving more 'uprightly' – would make the ball fly straighter.

Today, few top players or teachers would argue with the premise that the body must rotate at a shallower or 'flatter' angle than the arms swing up and down for the club to be consistently delivered to the ball with its face square to the target while travelling momentarily directly along the target line and at the correct angle of attack.

The reason, of course, is that attempting to swing excessively 'straight' generates in most people a 'rocking and blocking' action of the shoulders – a tilting rather than a rotational motion – that produces all kinds of mis-hits by forcing the hands, wrists, and arms to work independently of what the rest of the body is doing.

In the end, each of us at this game has to discover what works best for himself as an individual by hard experience – by plain trial and error within a framework of tried and tested fundamentals.

In that regard, I believe we are now at a stage in the evolution of the golf swing where combining **rotation** of the body with **upward and downward** swinging of the arms has become the universally accepted framework for that often frustrating but ever fascinating exercise.

LEE
TREVINO

IN THE END, EACH OF US AT
THIS GAME HAS TO
DISCOVER WHAT WORKS
BEST FOR OURSELVES AS
AN INDIVIDUAL BY HARD
EXPERIENCE – BY PLAIN
TRIAL AND ERROR WITHIN A
FRAMEWORK OF TRIED AND
TESTED FUNDAMENTALS.

CHAPTER 48
Golf at its simplest

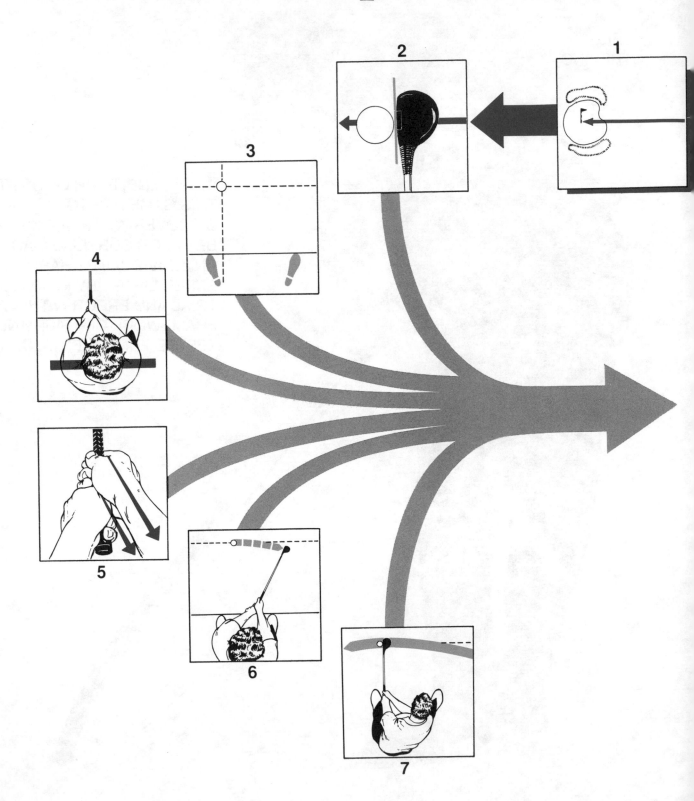

Q What's the simplest way to become a good golfer?

A To play this game really well, you must first understand and accept that you will never hit a golf ball exactly as you wish every time you swing. No one ever has and no one ever will. Two of the greatest golfers in history, Ben Hogan and Jack Nicklaus, regarded a round in which they hit four or five shots precisely as they intended an exceptionally fine one in terms of ball-striking.

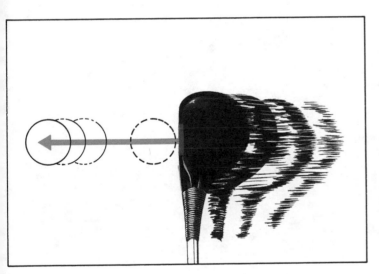

Nevertheless, your chances of **minimising the amount you miss by** – the key to *scoring* at golf – are definitely improved by *trying* to hit every shot perfectly. Here, then, as simply as I can express it, is the process that most easily and frequently produces perfect golf shots:

1. Select target and visualise shot flying to it.

2. Mind-picturing target and target line promotes correct clubface aiming.

3. Correct clubface aiming establishes proper ball positioning relative to feet.

4. Correct ball positioning promotes proper body alignment and posture.

5. Correct ball positioning and body alignment promote proper gripping.

6. Correct gripping, body alignment, and posture promote swinging club back in proper plane and direction.

7. Correct backswing promotes automatically swinging the clubhead through impact at maximum speed with clubface looking in same direction clubhead is travelling.

Golf has been such a wonderful game for me that I want everyone else who plays it to enjoy it as much.

I hope this book helps to achieve that goal.